4th Workshop on NLP for Computer Assisted Language Learning 2015

Held at NODALIDA 2015

NEALT Proceedings Series Volume 26

Vilnius, Lithuania
11-13 May 2015

Editors:

Elena Volodina
Ildiko Pilan
Lars Borin

ISBN: 978-1-5108-0298-8

Printed from e-media with permission by:

Curran Associates, Inc.
57 Morehouse Lane
Red Hook, NY 12571

Some format issues inherent in the e-media version may also appear in this print version.

Printed by Curran Associates, Inc. (2015)

For permission requests, please contact the Association for Computational Linguistics at the address below.

Association for Computational Linguistics
209 N. Eighth Street
Stroudsburg, Pennsylvania 18360

Phone: 1-570-476-8006
Fax: 1-570-476-0860

acl@aclweb.org

Additional copies of this publication are available from:

Curran Associates, Inc.
57 Morehouse Lane
Red Hook, NY 12571 USA
Phone: 845-758-0400
Fax: 845-758-2634
Email: curran@proceedings.com
Web: www.proceedings.com

NEALT

Northern European Association for Language Technology

NEALT Proceedings Series Vol. 26

Proceedings of the 4th Workshop on

NLP for Computer Assisted Language Learning

NODALIDA 2015

May 11-13, 2015
Institute of the Lithuanian Language
Vilnius, Lithuania

Proceedings of the

4th workshop on NLP for Computer Assisted Language Learning

at NODALIDA 2015
Vilnius, 11th May, 2015

edited by

Elena Volodina, Lars Borin and Ildikó Pilán

Preface

The workshop series on Natural Language Processing (NLP) for Computer-Assisted Language Learning (CALL) – NLP4CALL – is a meeting place for researchers working on the integration of Natural Language Processing and Speech Technologies in CALL systems and exploring the theoretical and methodological issues arising in this connection.

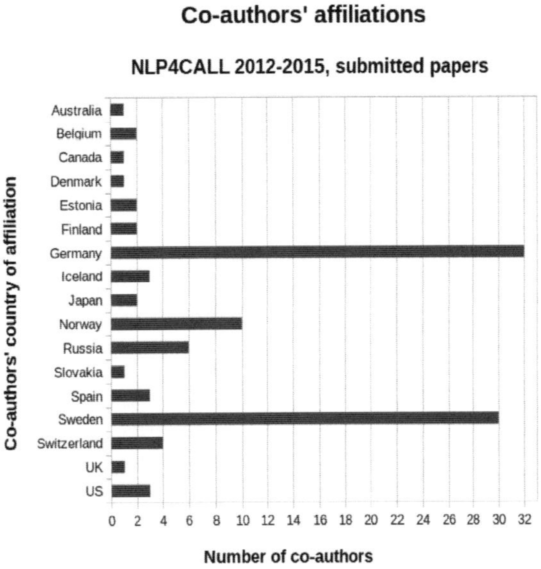

The first four editions of this workshop series[1] enjoyed have attracted participants from all over the world, including researchers from Australia, Canada, Central, South and Northern Europe, Russia as well as USA (see the figure on the right). The workshops have shown the vast potential that Language Technology holds for language learning and – most importantly – the interest that LT researchers have in the domain of CALL.

The intersection of Natural Language Processing and Speech Technology, with Computer-Assisted Language Learning (CALL) brings "understanding" of language to CALL tools, thus making CALL intelligent. This fact has provided the name for this area of research – Intelligent CALL, ICALL. As the definition suggests, apart from having excellent knowledge of Natural Language Processing and/or Speech Technology, ICALL researchers need good insights into second language acquisition (SLA) theories and practices, as well as knowledge of second language pedagogy and didactics. This workshop covers therefore all ICALL-relevant research areas, including studies where NLP-enriched tools are used for testing SLA and pedagogical theories, and vice versa, where SLA theories/pedagogical practices are modeled in ICALL tools.

This year we welcomed papers

- that describe research directly aimed at ICALL,
- that demonstrate actual or discuss potential use of existing Speech Technologies, NLP tools or resources for language learning,
- that describe ongoing development of resources and tools with potential usage in ICALL, either directly in interactive applications, or indirectly in materials, application or curriculum development, e.g. collecting and annotating ICALL-relevant corpora; developing tools and algorithms for readability analysis, selecting optimal corpus examples, etc.

1 <http://www.spraakbanken.gu.se/icall>

Elena Volodina, Lars Borin and Ildikó Pilán 2015. Preface. *Proceedings of the 4th workshop on NLP for Computer Assisted Language Learning at NODALIDA 2015.* NEALT Proceedings Series 26 / Linköping Electronic Conference Proceedings 114: i–iii.

- that discuss challenges and/or research agenda for ICALL
- we were also interested in software demonstrations

We especially invited submissions describing the above-mentioned themes for the Nordic languages.

Submissions to the four workshop editions have targeted a wide variety of languages, ranging from well-resourced languages (German, English, French, Russian, Spanish) to under-resourced ones (Estonian, Saami, Võro), among which several Nordic languages have been targeted: Danish, Estonian, Icelandic, Norwegian, Saami, Swedish, and Võro (see the figure to the right).

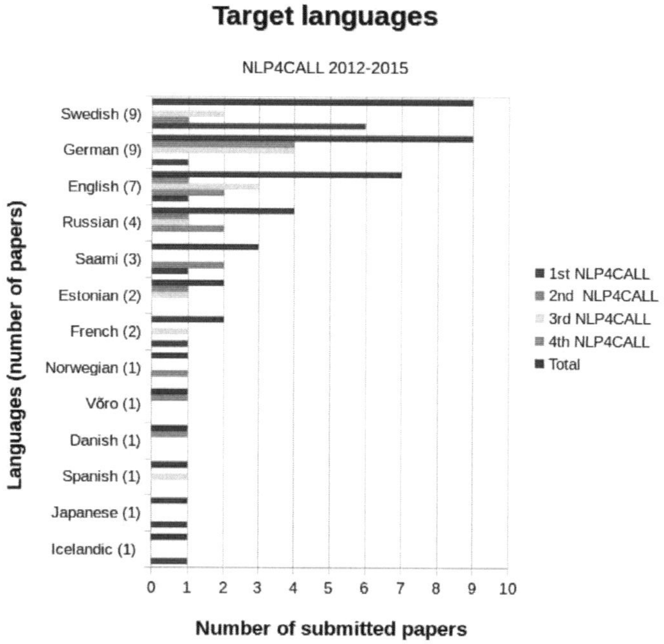

Up to date, the top 5 topics that have dominated the workshop submissions include the generation of language tests and exercises, readability studies, the generation of interactive feedback, the automatic scoring of essays and short answers, and error diagnosis (see more topics in the figure to the right).

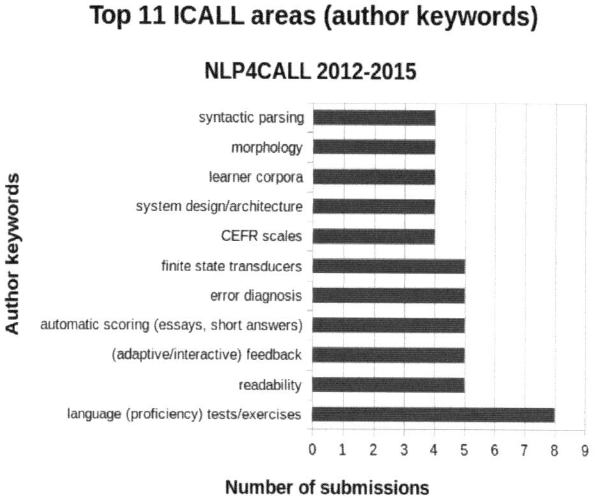

The workshop series on NLP for CALL is organized by a Special Interest Group on Intelligent Computer-Assisted Language Learning (SIG-ICALL of NEALT)[2], and it has received financial support from the Centre for Language Technology at the University of Gothenburg, Sweden (CLT)[3] .

2 <http://spraakbanken.gu.se/swe/forskning/ICALL/SIG-ICALL>

3 <http://clt.gu.se/>

We intend to continue this workshop series, which up to date has been the only ICALL-relevant recurring event based in the Nordic countries. Our intention is to co-locate the workshop series with the two major biennial LT events in Scandinavia, the Swedish Language Technology Conference, SLTC, and the Nordic Conference of Language Technology, NODALIDA, thus making this workshop an annual event. Through this workshop, we intend to profile ICALL research in the Nordic countries and to provide a dissemination venue for researchers active in this area.

Our special thanks go to the program committee members who have put in a major effort reviewing the submissions:

- Lars Ahrenberg, Linköping University, Sweden
- Eckhard Bick, University of Southern Denmark, Denmark
- Lars Borin, University of Gothenburg, Sweden
- Antonio Branco, University of Lisbon, Portugal
- Frederik Cornillie, KU Leuven Kulak, Belgium
- Piet Desmet, KU Leuven Kulak, Belgium
- Simon Dobnik, University of Gothenburg, Sweden
- Robert Eklund, Linköping University, Sweden
- Thomas François, UCLouvain, Belgium
- Katarina Heimann Mühlenbock, DART, Sahlgrenska Universitetssjukhuset, Sweden
- Kris Heylen, KU Leuven, Belgium
- Sofie Johansson Kokkinakis, University of Gothenburg, Sweden
- Chris Koniaris, University of Gothenburg, Sweden
- Staffan Larsson, University of Gothenburg, Sweden
- Montse Maritxalar, University of the Basque country, Spain
- Detmar Meurers, University of Tübingen, Germany
- Martí Quixal, University of Tübingen, Germany
- Martin Russell, University of Birmingham, UK
- Mathias Schulze, University of Waterloo, Canada
- Joel Tetreault, Yahoo! Labs, USA
- Trond Trosterud, Universitetet i Tromsø, Norway
- Cornelia Tschichold, Swansea University, UK
- Francis Tyers, The Arctic University of Norway, Norway
- Elena Volodina, University of Gothenburg, Sweden
- Robert Östling, Stockholm University, Sweden

The workshop organizers
Elena Volodina,
Lars Borin,
Ildikó Pilán

Workshop website: <http://spraakbanken.gu.se/eng/research/icall/4thnlp4call>

Acknowledgements:

Financial support for the organization of the workshop has come from the University of Gothenburg through its funding of the Centre for Language Technology: <http://www.clt.gu.se>

Contents

Preface i
Elena Volodina, Lars Borin and Ildikó Pilán

Misspellings in responses to listening comprehension questions: Prospects for scoring based on phonetic normalization 1
Heike Da Silva Cardoso and Magdalena Wolska

Taking the Danish Speech Trainer from CALL to ICALL 11
Peter Juel Henrichsen

Using shallow syntactic features to measure influences of L1 and proficiency level in EFL writings 21
Andrea Horbach, Jonathan Poitz and Alexis Palmer

Semi-automated typical error annotation for learner English essays: Integrating frameworks 35
Andrey Kutuzov and Elizaveta Kuzmenko

Short answer grading: When sorting helps and when it doesn't 42
Ulrike Pado and Cornelia Kiefer

Oahpa! Õpi! Opiq! Developing free online programs for learning Estonian and Võro 51
Heli Uibo, Jaak Pruulmann-Vengerfeldt, Jack Rueter and Sulev Iva

Misspellings in Responses to Listening Comprehension Questions: Prospects for Scoring based on Phonetic Normalization

Heike da Silva Cardoso[†] and **Magdalena Wolska**[*]
[†]Department of Linguistics [*]LEAD Graduate School
Eberhard Karls Universität Tübingen, Tübingen, Germany
{hcardoso,magdalena.wolska}@uni-tuebingen.de

Abstract

Automated scoring systems which evaluate content require robust ways of dealing with form errors. The work presented in this paper is set in the context of scoring learners' responses to listening comprehension items included in a placement test of German as a foreign language. Based on a corpus of over 3000 responses to 17 questions, by test takers of different language proficiencies, we perform a quantitative analysis of the diversity in misspellings. We evaluate the performance of an off-the-shelf open source spell-checker on our data showing that around 45% of the reported non-word errors are not correctly accounted for, that is, they are either falsely identified as misspelt or the spell-checker is unable to identify the intended word.

We propose to address misspellings in computer-based scoring of constructed response items by means of phonetic normalization. Learner responses transcribed into Soundex codes and into two encodings borrowed from historical linguistics (ASJP and Dolgopolsky's sound classes) are compared to transcribed reference answers using string distance measures. We show that reliable correlation with teachers' scores can be obtained, however, similarity thresholds are item-specific.

1 Introduction

Form errors are the type of noise in linguistic data that can interfere with computational language analysis already at the preprocessing stage. Form errors in writing range from basic mechanics errors, such as capitalization or punctuation errors, through spelling and word-formation errors (which in many cases cannot be clearly differentiated), up to sentence structure, syntactic, errors. In this paper we address one class of form errors, non-word misspellings, in the context of a semantics-oriented task: assessment of constructed responses to German as a Foreign Language listening comprehension questions.

In the task of content scoring, misspellings introduce obvious noise. A recently proposed method of addressing the spelling problem in *automated* scoring involves phonetic normalization based on Soundex, a coarse-granularity sound-based coding. Shedeed (2011) used Soundex in a system for scoring short answers in Arabic. Hahn et al. (2013) used an analogous method for German and showed that a bag-of-Soundex model outperforms other models on unseen data at the accuracy over 85%.

The work presented here has been motivated by a different approach to content scoring: *computer-assisted* scoring. In the context of a real-world task, instead of automatically assigning scores we group responses that are likely to be graded with the same scores with the goal of streamlining manual scoring (see (Wolska et al., 2014)). Identifying responses that are similar at the appropriate level of abstraction is thus crucial here. In the study presented in this paper, we evaluate the prospects for using phonetic string encodings based on sound classes derived in historical linguistics as a preprocessing step for this task.

In historical and comparative linguistics sound classes are used, among others to detect cognates, identify relatedness among languages, or detect or explain changes in sound patterns. Phonetic encoding in this case is a normalization step which serves to make languages comparable. In our case, phonetic normalization of type-written responses to *listening* comprehension items is motivated by the fact that students, especially those of lower

[*]Corresponding author

Heike Da Silva Cardoso and Magdalena Wolska 2015. Misspellings in responses to listening comprehension questions: Prospects for scoring based on phonetic normalization. *Proceedings of the 4th workshop on NLP for Computer Assisted Language Learning at NODALIDA 2015.* NEALT Proceedings Series 26 / Linköping Electronic Conference Proceedings 114: 1–10.

proficiency, tend to misspell words to some extent in systematic ways, for instance, related to the properties of their mother-tongue (orthography rules or phonological differences between the mother-tongue and the target language).

Based on a corpus of learner responses to listening comprehension items, in this paper we answer the following questions:

- What is the extent of the misspellings problem in learner responses to German listening comprehension questions?
- How diverse are misspellings, that is, to what extent they diverge from target hypotheses?
- To what extent an off-the-shelf spell-checking tool can "solve" the problem?
- Does grouping responses based on phonetic normalization account for teacher's response scores?

In the context of the last question, we test two linguistically-motivated phonetic encodings of different granularity: ASJPcode (Wichmann et al., 2013) and Dolgopolsky's classes (Dolgopolsky, 1986). These are compared to Soundex encoding (Russell, 1918 1922), a practically-motivated indexing method, which, as mentioned earlier, had been previously proposed as a preprocessing step in content scoring. We hypothesize that normalization based on the linguistically-motivated systems should yield response groups that better reflect the assigned scores than grouping based on Soundex encoding.

2 Related Work

Research into misspellings in learner language has been predominantly addressing English as the target (see, for instance, (Flor and Futagi, 2012) for a recent overview). Analogous lines of work based on digital corpora has been emerging for German as a Foreign Language. Rimrott and Heift (2008) analyzed the performance of MS Word spell-checker on learner German and found that around 20% of misspellings were undetected. For single-error words, in over 40% of the cases the correct word was not in the suggestion list whereas for multiple-error words in about 80% of the cases the spell-checker failed to provide a correction. In a further study, Heift and Rimrott (2008) found that in CALL activities students are influenced by a word's position in the list of suggestions when they select an alternative spelling. Clearly, with incorrect top-level suggestions, only more errors are introduced.

Corpus-based studies into low-level form errors in German learner writing are sparse. Boyd (2010) created a corpus of online workbook exercises and essays submitted of by American students learning German and built a subcorpus of around 1200 non-word spelling errors found in this data. The most prominent error annotated German learner corpus is Falko (Reznicek et al., 2013) and it also includes annotations of target hypotheses for misspellings. Juozulynas (2013) analyzed around 350 German essays written by American college students and found that around 15% of the identified errors were spelling errors. Analysis of accuracy of robust automated correction was not performed in these studies.

To our knowledge, the only prior work in which explicit phonetic normalization is employed in content scoring is the previously mentioned work by Shedeed (2011) and the subsequent study by Hahn et al. (2013). In both cases Soundex coding is used.

3 Listening Comprehension Corpus

Data collection In this study we used responses to listening comprehension (LC) items collected during placement tests for language courses (four cohorts of students) administered by the Saarland University's International Office centre for Teaching German as a Foreign Language. The tests consisted of three parts: grammar, C-Test, and listening comprehension. The listening part consisted of three audio stimuli of increasing difficulty in terms of linguistic properties and speech tempo. The stimuli were accompanied with up to 11 constructed response questions each. For each question the teachers provided one or more correct reference answers.

The tests were developed by an experienced teacher of the language centre and conducted using a web-based platform. Students' responses, preprocessed as outlined below, were scored manually – for the most part one teacher, head of the centre – also using a web-based platform. Responses were graded on a [0,1] or [0,2] scale; half points were used for partial credits. Approximately 600 students of various proficiencies and mother tongues participated in the tests.

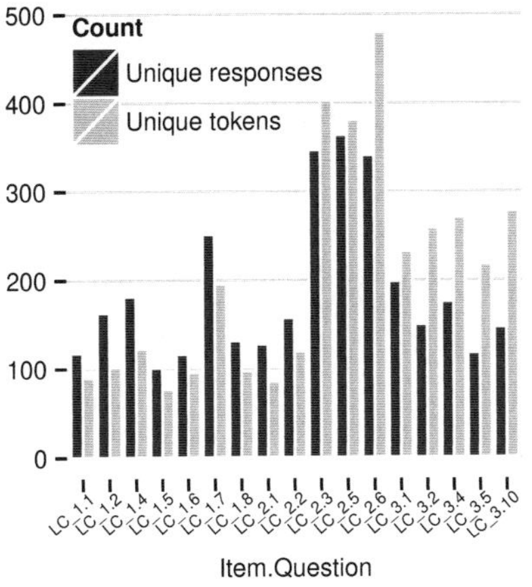

Figure 1: Number of unique responses and unique tokens per question

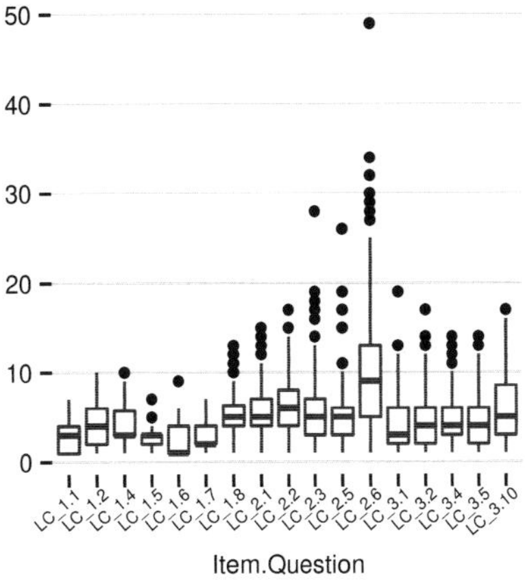

Figure 2: Response lengths, in tokens, per question

Variable	N
Verbatim responses	7208
Verbatim unique	3794
Preprocessed unique	3146
Tokens	16298
Token types	2429

Table 1: Descriptive corpus information

Preprocessing Certain minor form errors, such as wrong capitalization or irregular punctuation, are irrelevant while assessing comprehension. We exploit this in a scoring platform to reduce the set of responses to score by normalizing spurious writing mechanics differences which are not considered score-affecting in assessing comprehension. This includes lower-casing and removing clause- and sentence-final punctuation. In order to avoid differences in edit distance due to diacritics use, we also transcribe umlaut characters, using the standard convention, with their underlying vowel followed by 'e' ('ö' as 'oe', 'ü' as 'ue', etc.). Preprocessing reduces the set of responses which teachers need to score by more than 50% for some items. For this study we use responses scored in the preprocessed form. For the analysis presented in this paper we use a subset of the scored preprocessed responses selected as summarized below.

The corpus Since the number of responses differs from question to question (at least partially due to different language proficiencies of the test-takers; low-proficiency test-takers are not capable of responding to questions to the more difficult audio prompts) and for some questions it is low (only 29 responses to one of the questions after preprocessing) for the analyses presented in this paper, we selected only those questions to which we have at least 100 unique preprocessed responses. We moreover excluded questions which elicited unordered multi-part responses, that is, questions of the type "Name 3 ..." or "What are ...? (2 items)". Our complete data set consists of responses to 17 questions which elicited single-part responses and each response has been scored at 0, 0.5, or 1 points.

Table 1 shows basic descriptive information about the corpus. The number of verbatim responses is the total number of responses to the 17 questions before preprocessing. "Verbatim unique" is the number of token-identical verbatim responses collapsed to one observation. "Preprocessed unique" is the number of token-identical (unique) responses after preprocessing as described in the previous paragraph. "Tokens" and "Token types" are, respectively, the number of all tokens and unique tokens (types) in the preprocessed responses.

In the remainder of this paper, we refer to the set of preprocessed unique responses. Figure 1 shows the distribution of responses and unique tokens per question for the three items (LC_1, LC_2, LC_3). Figure 2 shows the distribution of response lengths per question. There are more unique responses to the more difficult items, LC_2 and LC_3, and the responses to those items are longer and more di-

LC_1.1	LC_1.6	LC_3.1
frankreisch	austereich	giespallampe
frankrich	austerreich	energiespaerlaempe
frankriech	oestereicht	energysparen
frankrreisch	oeustreich	energiesparenlampen
frankrreit	ostreich	energiesparlampel
franzoezisch	oesterreisch	energiesparer
franzuezisch	oesttereich	energiespannlampe
freinkreich	oeustreich	energisparelampen
frienkriesch	oeschterich	sparrlampen
frienricht	oessterrisch	energiespaerlaempe

Figure 3: Examples of misspelled responses

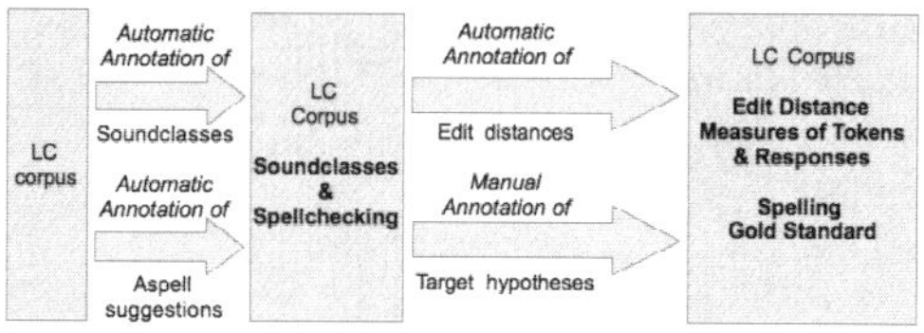

Figure 4: Corpus processing

verse (the number of unique tokens larger than the number of unique responses, that is, fewer recurring words than in the easiest item, LC_1). The average response length was 5 tokens.

Examples In order to illustrate the spelling errors problem, in Figure 3 we show examples of misspellings in responses to three questions which elicited simple one-word key concepts. We will use responses to these questions in one of the analyses (RAs below are reference answers provided by the teachers; vertical bar separates alternatives):

LC_1.1 Wo wohnt Alexandra?
'Where does Alexandra live?'
RA: frankreich

LC_1.6 Woher kommt Elisabeth?
'Where does Elisabeth come from?'
RA: oesterreich|wien|wien oesterreich

LC_3.1 Wie beleuchtet die Bundeskanzlerin Angela Merkel ihre Wohnung?
'How does Chancellor Angela Merkel light her apartment'
RA: energiesparlampen
'energy saving lamps'

Two of the questions (LC_1.1 and LC_1.6) appeared with the first, easiest, listening prompt. Even though identifying the answers within the audio prompts was easy for most test-takers, also low-proficiency, spelling the answers correctly turned out to be challenging, even though the elicited key concepts denote two well known European countries. The third question (LC_3.1) appeared with the last, most difficult, audio prompt and was answered by medium- to high-proficiency learners. Likewise here spelling the word is challenging. This may be partially due to the fact that "Energiesparlampe" is a compound noun.

Even this small sample illustrates the large variety of spelling errors, the high complexity of the spell-checking task, and the high demands on automated processing. Some misspellings, such as *lampel* for "lampe" or "lampen", are probably typos, while others are likely to have a phonological source, like *frankreisch* or *oesterreisch*, and among those some might be explained by interference of another foreign or the native language of the student, for instance "au" in *austereich* or "y" in *energysparen*. Some errors might be interpreted as wrong morphological forms rather than misspellings, e.g. *energisparelampen*. In many cases multiple errors are combined.

4 Spell-checking and Normalizations

As shown in Figure 4, data for analysis was prepared as follows: We created a spelling gold-standard semi-automatically by spell-checking preprocessed responses using an off-the-shelf spell-checker (described in more details in Section 4.1) and then manually annotating (verifying and correcting) the checker's outputs (Section 4.2). Each learner response and reference answer was automatically transcribed into three different phonetically-based encodings which, in the context of the automated scoring task, we treat as spelling normalizations (Section 4.3). In the analysis section we compare the spell-checked and the phonetically transcribed responses with, respectively, the strings or the transcriptions of target hypotheses and reference answers. The methods and tools used for annotation and normalization are outlined below.

4.1 Spell-checking

For automated spell-checking and spelling correction we use Aspell (Atkinson, 2006), an open source spell-checker provided by GNU. Aspell supports multiple languages and is frequently used as a reference system in research on spell-checking and writing normalization. Crucially to this work, a large dictionary for the German language compatible with Aspell is freely available, as are implementations of the system itself. Aspell is thus a good candidate for integration into a scoring system, and so a well-motivated choice for an evaluation.

Aspell performs checking and suggests corrections based on a combination of orthographic and phonetic coding, fast dictionary lookup, and an edit distance calculation. Alternative spellings are identified by an algorithm which represents words by their orthographic forms and their "soundslike" equivalents, that is, approximate pronunciations constructed based on phonetic information. Suggestions are ordered by a weighted average of the edit distances between the candidate and the misspelled word and between the "soundslike" encodings of the two words. Aspell language versions differ in their dictionaries and phonetic data, but the underlying edit distance algorithm is the same.

Note that Aspell performs context-insensitive spell-checking, that is, individual words are processed in isolation. Thus, only non-word errors are detected, while real-word errors are not. In this study we do not address real-word errors, however, we are planning to annotate the complete data set manually in the future.

4.2 Annotation

We annotated the learner responses with target hypotheses (hypothesized intended forms) semi-automatically using the Aspell checker. For each non-word Aspell searches its dictionary and provides a list of suggested replacements. To obtain a spell-checked corpus we processed our data set with Aspell and for each word which Aspell reported as misspelled, we stored Aspell's first suggestion. Then, we manually checked the first suggestions and corrected them were necessary.

As Figure 3 illustrates, the range of spelling variants includes cases of questionable interpretation and acceptability; consider, for instance, *frienricht* or *giespallampe* as misspellings of "frankreich" and "energiesparlampe", respectively. When building the spelling gold standard we did not use the teachers' scores as guides, but rather attempted to accept generously those words which could be in good faith interpreted to be misspellings of the expected concepts. Where good-faith interpretation was impossible or borderline possible, we marked those words as uninterpretable (for instance, *frankaise, freikeit, franch* in response to LC_1.1 and *oestech, busterish, uscraisch*, or *susthei* in response to LC_1.6). We also marked foreign words explicitly (*france, francais, austria*) as some students answered in English or in their native language.

The annotation was carried out by the authors of this paper. The corpus was divided into parts and single annotation was performed for each misspelled word by one author. The manually corrected spell-checker outputs are used as a spelling gold standard. The spell-checked, annotated corpus contains 2945 responses, 15260 tokens (2898 unique responses, 2173 unique tokens).

4.3 String Normalizations

For this study we used three phonetically-based encodings: ASJP and Dolgopolsky's systems, and Soundex as baseline.

ASJPcode Automated Similarity Judgment Program (ASJP) is a procedure originating from comparative and historical linguistics developed with the view to comparing world languages by lexical similarity (Wichmann et al., 2013). Comparisons are based on word lists encoded in standardized orthography (ASJPcode), a simplified version of the International Phonetic Alphabet (International Phonetic Association, 1999). ASJP encoding consists of 41 symbols, 7 vowels and 34 consonants, which represent the commonly occurring sounds of the world's languages (for details, see Appendix C of (Brown et al., 2008)). The transcription employed in this study was specifically designed to capture the sound representations of German.

Dolgopolsky's sound classes The sound class coding system of Dolgopolsky (1986) was developed in the context of research analogous to the ASJP project, that of identifying related language families. Dolgopolsky's system groups similar consonants into 10 "sound classes" in such way that phonetic regularities within a class are more systematic than between classes. Each class is represented with a single character. Vowels are simply marked as such (V). The transcription used in this study was also designed to capture the sound system of German.

String	ASJP	Dolgopolsky	Soundex
frankeriech	fGaNkeGiS	PRVNKVRVS	F652
frankfurt	fGaNkfuGt	PRVNKPVRT	F652
fraenkerisch	fGaENkeGiS	PRVVNKVRVS	F652
fracraich	fGakGaiS	PRVKRVVS	F626
oestarreich	7oEstaGaiS	HVVSTVRVVS	O236
oestereisch	7oEsteGaiS	HVVSTVRVVS	O236
austerreich	7austEGaiS	HVVSTVRVVS	A236
austerreicht	7austEGaiSt	HVVSTVRVVST	A236

Figure 5: Examples of normalizations

Both ASJP and Dolgopolsky's transcriptions were done based on sound classes for German as is done in the LingPy package (List and Moran, 2013; List et al., 2013).

Soundex Soundex, originally patented by Russell (1918 1922), also uses sound classes to represent similar sounding words with the same encoding, however, it was designed with a practical goal of indexing family names for the census. A Soundex code represents a token with a character followed by three digits. The character denotes the first letter of the word and the digits denote the sound classes of the three following consonants. There are six such sound classes. Vowels, unless word-initial, are ignored, as are the letters H and W. If the word is longer than the four symbol sequence, the remaining letters are ignored. If it is shorter, zeros are added. Soundex is thus a more general approach than the other two and most lossy (to a greater degree abstracts away from the original string), but as it is one of the most frequently employed phonetic encodings and therefore a good baseline for comparison. Soundex has been also used in previous work on short answer scoring as a way of addressing misspellings (Hahn et al., 2013).

To illustrate the selected phonetic normalizations, examples of encoding are shown in Figure 5. As can be clearly seen, the effect of the normalizations is markedly different and reflects the more linguistically-informed basis of the ASJP and Dolgopolsky's codes: In the set of responses to LC_1.1, *frankeriech*, *fraenkerisch*, and *frankfurt* are grouped into one sound equivalence class by Soundex – an undesired result – but not by any of the other encodings. In the set of responses to LC_1.6, *oestarreich*, *oestereisch* and *austerreich*, *austerreicht* form two clusters in Soundex encoding, whereas ASJP and Dolgopolsky's codes yield more intuitive groupings; ASJP being more fine-grained than Dolgopolsky.

	Valid words	Misspelled words	Row totals
Reported	42	1040	1082
Suggestions found	21	904	925
First Correct	-	583	583
First Wrong	21	321	342
No Suggestions	21	136	157

Table 2: Performance of the Aspell spell-checker

5 Results

The following analyses are performed: We start by summarizing the performance of the spell-checker at the word-level. Next, we look at the extent of divergence of the misspelled words from the annotated target hypotheses by quantifying divergence in terms of string distances. Then, we relate misspellings and normalizations to scores: For two questions eliciting single key concept responses, we show how distance to the key concepts affects response scores. Finally, we focus on complete responses and look at relations between scores and distances between normalized learner responses and reference responses.

Two standard string distance measures are used throughout this section: Damerau-Levenshtein distance (nDL), a variant of Levenshtein edit distance which accounts for transposition of adjacent characters (Damerau, 1964; Levenshtein, 1966), and string vector cosine based on n-grams. A length correction on the edit distance is performed in a standard way by dividing the distance by the length of the longer string. Cosine similarity is computed for unigrams, bigrams and trigrams. Because the data is not normally distributed and for some items the number of observations is low, instead of performing statistical analysis, we present boxplots to show general tendencies in an informative way.

5.1 Automated Spell-checking

The performance of the Aspell spell-checker against the gold-standard is summarized in Table 2. "Valid words" refers to correctly spelled words and "Misspelled words" to non-words. The numbers refer to *unique* tokens.

Out of the 2173 unique tokens, Aspell reported around 50% (1082) as misspelled. Since there were 1818 occurrences of misspellings overall, it is clear that a lot of the same misspellings recur. Out of the 1082 reported misspellings

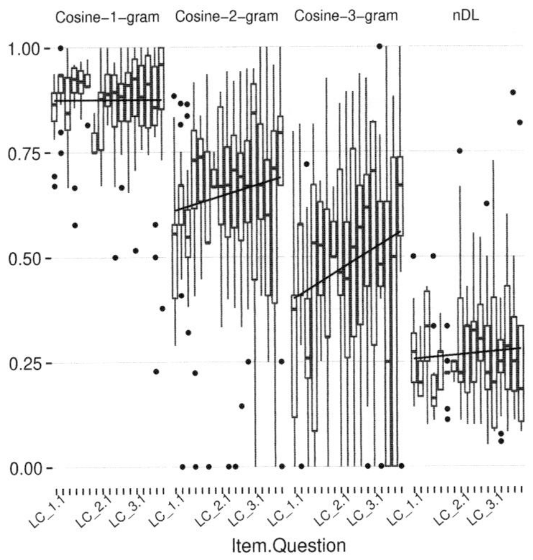

Figure 6: Per item distribution of distances between misspelled words and target hypotheses

Aspell reported 21 (4%) correctly spelled words as misspelled and suggested a correction (false positives). Overall Aspell's precision in identifying misspellings in our data is thus at 96%.[1]

Now, as far as automated correction is concerned, suggestions were found for not even 60% of the tokens. Out of the 925 tokens for which suggestions were found, 321 first suggestions were wrong, yielding a false negative rate of 64%. With 321 wrong suggestions and 136 cases for which suggestions were not available, about 45% of the non-word misspellings are not accounted for correctly by Aspell. These results are similar to those reported by Rimrott and Heift (2008).

A major issue for Aspell, and, as can be expected, for any off-the-shelf German spell-checker, are compound nouns. Two of the listening prompts contained compounds as key concepts: "Marxhaus" in the answer to *Where are Peter and Birgit?* (RA: 'In front of Marx' birth place in Trier') and "Energiesparlampen" in the answer to the previously mentioned LC_3.1. "Marxhaus" is not in Aspell's dictionary; the closest suggestions it finds as replacements include *Matthäus* (Matthew; as in Matthew the Apostle), *Parkhaus* (carpark) or even *Hausbar* (house bar). Compounds account for all the 21 valid words which Aspell identified as misspellings.

[1]We cannot provide recall results at this point since our gold standard includes only non-words identified by Aspell. We are planning to annotate real-word errors in the future.

Most of the remaining errors are due to context insensitivity; for instance, to "What did Karl Marx do in Cologne?" (RA: "Leitung der Neuen Rheinischen Zeitung" ('Led the "New Rhinish Newspaper"') a student wrote: *radikal demochratisch behzatung* ('radical democratic UNINTERPRETABLE') for which Aspell suggested *radikal demokratische Beratung* (radical democratic counseling) which considering pure edit distance obviously makes sense, otherwise not.

5.2 Diversity of Misspellings

Figure 6 shows the distribution of cosine and normalized Damerau-Levenshtein distances (nDL) to target hypotheses with linear trend lines. On the x-axis, items within distance measure groups are ordered as in Figures 1 and 2. As can be seen in the plots, the range of unigram cosine values is large for some items. Thus a lot of misspellings involve more than just letter transpositions. The large ranges in bigram cosines and many values at 0 for trigrams show that misspellings tend to diverge from the target hypotheses to a large extent.

For the easier questions (left end of the x subaxes) the ranges of unigram cosine and Levenshtein distance tend to be smaller, while bigram and trigram cosines are larger and they are also closer to the low-end of the scale. This means that in the easy questions, misspellings tend to contain the right letters, but the letters are misplaced. The same can be seen for the difficult questions (except for the last one). The intermediate difficulty items tend to have the least letter overlap and many trigram similarities at the low end of the scale. These are likely to be most difficult to correct automatically, but possibly easier to identify as qualifying to be scored at 0.

5.3 Relation to Scores: Misspelled Key Concepts

As mentioned in Section 3, we used responses to two questions which elicited one key concept, LC_1.1 and LC_1.6, to investigate the relation between misspellings and scores. From the LC_1.1-LC_1.6 corpus subset, we extracted responses which contained tokens with gold standard annotation corresponding to the expected concept: "frankreich" for LC_1.1 and "oesterreich" for LC_1.6. There were 236 and 260 such responses, respectively.

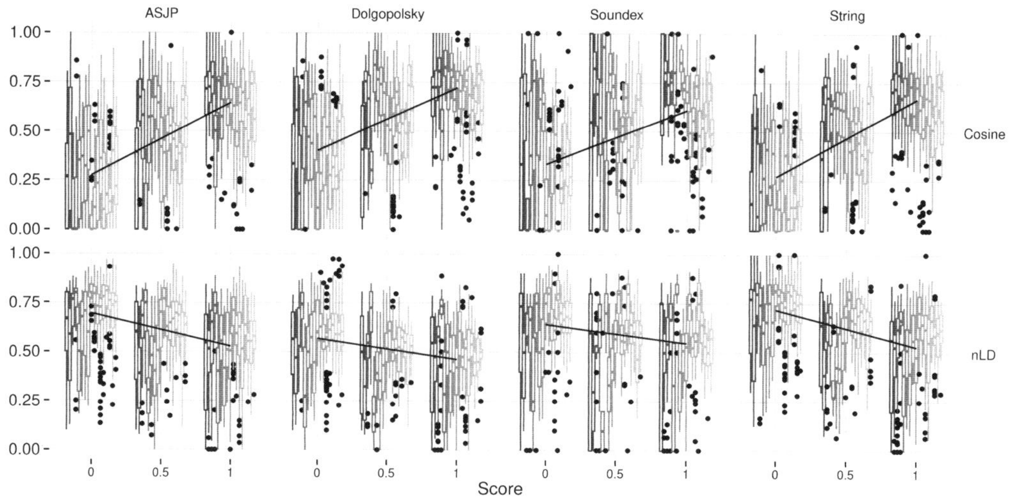

Figure 8: Per score distribution of distances between normalized responses and reference responses

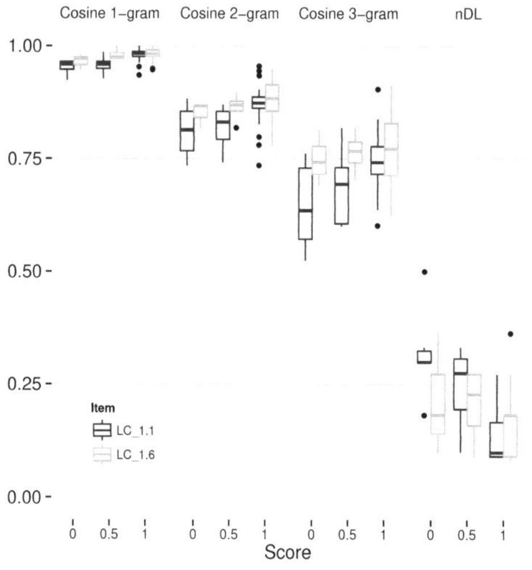

Figure 7: Per score distribution of distances between misspelled key concepts and target hypotheses for two items

For these responses, in Figure 7 we show the distribution of the distances to the target hypotheses between score points.

Most of the expected general tendencies can be found in the data: cosine distances for all n-grams increase with the scores as expected. Levenshtein distance decreases as expected for LC_1.1, but the pattern for LC_1.6 is not clear. Moreover, and more interestingly, the acceptability thresholds for the two questions appear to be different. Responses with misspelled key tokens of lower similarity to the target concept tokens are accepted with partial and full scores in LC_1.1. Also a larger range of similarity accounts for partial and full points in LC_1.1. This suggests that what counts as acceptable in terms of misspellings could be item-specific and different thresholds would have to be used for different items.

5.4 Relation to Scores: Normalizations

Finally, we investigate the relation between sound class-based response normalizations and the scores assigned by teachers. Complete preprocessed learner and reference responses have been transcribed into the three encodings described in Section 4.3. Based on Figure 7 the 3-gram cosine distance yields a pattern that best distinguishes between the three score points. Therefore, only 3-gram cosine distances are reported for the normalized responses. We seek to find out which normalization yields the most consistent patterns in terms of the expected relation to the teachers' scores.

The distributions of distances between normalized learner and reference responses for all the items are shown in Figure 8. Items clustered by score-point are ordered as in Figures 1 and 2. Distribution of string distances is shown for comparison. Linear trends are overlayed.

Two immediate observations can be made of the results. First, the score-based grouping is not clear-cut and the distance ranges overlap across score levels. Second, the expected pattern of cosine distance (linearly) increasing and normalized

Levenshtein distance (linearly) decreasing can be seen in the distribution of ASJP and Dolgopolsky normalizations, but less so in the distribution of Soundex distances across items. Soundex transcriptions do not distinguish well between the scores based on Levenshtein distance and only somewhat better based on cosine; for most items there is little difference between mean distances for scores 0.5 and 1 on the nLD measure and between mean scores 0.5 and 1. ASJP and Dolgopolsky normalizations are more stable in terms of variance, with ASJP, moreover, displaying fewer outliers. This confirms our hypothesis that the more linguistically-informed encoding yields clusters which better correspond to the assigned scores. It also suggests that these encodings might result in better performance on the automated scoring task. We are planning to investigate this in the course of further work. The ASJP and Dolgopolsky distributions moreover better reflect the pattern of string-based distances than the Soundex distributions. Finally, ASJP and Dolgopolsky normalizations appear more stable across items on both distance measures and the shape of the distributions is similar. It is possibly a combination of both that would work best as features for scoring.

6 Conclusions and Further Work

We presented a study on misspellings in a corpus of constructed responses to listening comprehension items used for placement testing for German. Not surprisingly, our data contains a large number of misspellings (around 50% of the unique words that learners used). The first-ranked suggestions of an off-the-shelf spell-checker were correct in not even 60% of the cases. This is likely to be partially due to the fact that the range of divergence from target forms is substantial. It also varies between questions. The majority of false positives were due to compounds specific to the listening prompts. An obvious solution we are pursuing to improve precision and reduce false negative suggestion rate is constructing two dictionaries: one prompt-specific and the other learner-language specific; the purpose of the latter is to provide prompt-specific frequent invalid forms produced by the learners.

We have also shown that while in general the expected trend in scoring misspelled responses can be observed, however, acceptability of divergence from target forms appears to be item-specific. Finally, we proposed sound class-based normalizations as a method of grouping noisy responses in terms of their pronunciation similarity as well as related distances between normalized responses and reference answers to response scores. This served to evaluate prospects for a normalization-based approach to response clustering. Soundex, the most frequently employed normalization, does not distinguish between responses at different score-points, so it can be considered the worst choice for a normalization-based approach. Both of the more elaborate phonetic transcriptions, based on ASJP's and Dolgopolsky's codes, perform better than Soundex and are promising directions to pursue. We will experiment with including distances to reference answers based on both representations as features for (semi-)automated scoring.

Acknowledgments

We thank Dr. Kristin Stezano Cotelo from the Saarland University International Office for collaboration on placement testing thanks to which this research is possible. We would like to thank Johannes Dellert for letting us use his code for sound class-based normalizations. We also thank the three anonymous reviewers for their helpful comments.

This work was funded by the Ministry of Science, Research and the Arts of Baden-Württemberg within the FRESCO project. Magdalena Wolska is supported by the Institutional Strategy of the University of Tübingen (Deutsche Forschungsgemeinschaft, ZUK 63).

References

Kevin Atkinson. 2006. Gnu Aspell 0.60.7. `http://aspell.net`.

Adriane Boyd. 2010. EAGLE: an Error-Annotated Corpus of Beginning Learner German. In *Proceedings of the 7th LREC*. `http://www.lrec-conf.org/proceedings/lrec2010/summaries/812`.

Cecil H Brown, Eric W Holman, Søren Wichmann, and Viveka Velupillai. 2008. Automated classification of the world's languages: a description of the method and preliminary results. *STUF-Language Typology and Universals Sprachtypologie und Universalienforschung*, 61(4):285–308. doi:10.1524/stuf.2008.0026.

Fred J. Damerau. 1964. A technique for computer detection and correction of spelling errors. *Communications of the ACM*. doi:10.1145/363958.363994.

Aharon B. Dolgopolsky. 1986. A probabilistic hypothesis concerning the oldest relationships among the language families of northern Eurasia. In *Typology, Relationship and Time: A Collection of Papers on Language Change and Relationship by Soviet Linguists*, pages 27–50. (Original: 1964 In: *Voprosy Jazykoznanija* 2).

Michael Flor and Yoko Futagi. 2012. On using context for automatic correction of non-word misspellings in student essays. In *Proceedings of the 7th Workshop on Building Educational Applications Using NLP*. `http://dl.acm.org/citation.cfm?id=2390397`.

Michael Hahn, Niels Ott, Ramon Ziai, and Detmar Meurers. 2013. CoMeT: Integrating different levels of linguistic modeling for meaning assessment. `https://aclweb.org/anthology/S/S13/S13-2102.pdf`.

Trude Heift and Anne Rimrott. 2008. Learner responses to corrective feedback for spelling errors in CALL. *System*. doi:10.1016/j.system.2007.09.007.

International Phonetic Association, editor. 1999. *Handbook of the International Phonetic Association: A guide to the use of the International Phonetic Alphabet*. Cambridge University Press.

Vilius Juozulynas. 2013. Errors in the compositions of second-year german students: An empirical study for parser-based icali. *CALICO Journal*. `https://ns.calico.org/html/article_578.pdf`.

V.I. Levenshtein. 1966. Binary codes capable of correcting deletions, insertions and reversals. *Soviet physics doklady*, 10(8):707–710.

Johann-Mattis List and Steven Moran. 2013. An open source toolkit for quantitative historical linguistics. In *Proceedings of the ACL Conference (System Demonstrations)*. `https://www.aclweb.org/anthology/P/P13/P13-4003.pdf`.

Johann-Mattis List, Steven Moran, Peter Bouda, and Johannes Dellert. 2013. LingPy. Python Library for Automatic Tasks in Historical Linguistics. `http://www.lingpy.org`.

Marc Reznicek, Anke Lüdeling, and Hagen Hirschmann. 2013. Competing target hypotheses in the Falko corpus. In *Automatic Treatment and Analysis of Learner Corpus Data*, volume 59 of *Studies in Corpus Linguistics*, pages 101–123.

Anne Rimrott and Trude Heift. 2008. Evaluating automatic detection of misspellings in German. *Language Learning & Technology*, 12(3):73–92. `http://llt.msu.edu/vol12num3/rimrottheift.pdf`.

Robert C. Russell. 1918, 1922. US Patents No.: 1261167 and 1435663. (Retrieved 04/15 via `http://patft.uspto.gov/netahtml/PTO/search-adv.htm`).

Howida A. Shedeed. 2011. A new intelligent methodology for computer based assessment of short answer question based on a new enhanced soundex phonetic algorithm for arabic language. *International Journal of Computer Applications*. `http://research.ijcaonline.org/volume34/number10/pxc3876054.pdf`.

Søren Wichmann, André Mller, Annkathrin Wett, Viveka Velupillai, Julia Bischoffberger, Cecil H. Brown, Eric W. Holman, Sebastian Sauppe, Zarina Molochieva, Pamela Brown, Harald Hammarström, Oleg Belyaev, Johann-Mattis List, Dik Bakker, Dmitry Egorov, Matthias Urban, Robert Mailhammer, Agustina Carrizo, Matthew S. Dryer, Evgenia Korovina, David Beck, Helen Geyer, Pattie Epps, Anthony Grant, and Pilar Valenzuela. 2013. The ASJP-Database (version 16). `http://asjp.clld.org` (Retrieved 04/15).

Magdalena Wolska, Andrea Horbach, and Alexis Palmer. 2014. Computer-assisted scoring of short responses: the efficiency of a clustering-based approach in a real-life task. In *Advances in Natural Language Processing (Proceedings of the 9th International Conference on Natural Language Processing (PolTAL-14))*. doi:10.1007/978-3-319-10888-9_31.

Taking the Danish Speech Trainer from CALL to ICALL

Peter Juel Henrichsen
DanCAST - Danish Center for Applied Speech Technology
Copenhagen Business School
pjh.ibc@cbs.dk

Abstract

Talebob (*Speech Bob*) is a newly developed interactive CALL-tool for training Danish speech with special regard to the pronunciation of highly idiomatic phrases. Talebob is currently being tested in primary schools in Nuuk, Hafnarfjörður and Tórshavn (where Danish is taught as a L2). The purpose of the current paper is twofold. We first introduce Talebob in its publicly available version, commenting on its linguistic, technical, and didactic principles. Secondly, we present our current plans and goals for the next version of Talebob focusing on linguistic and educational perspectives. Taking Talebob II as a point of departure, we wish to invite a discussion of ICALL as a means of modernizing the L2 educational programmes in the Nordic area.

1 Introduction

"Modern children crave to be watched and heard continuously", "Today's youth bore too easily", "The very ability to concentrate is crumbling in the young generation". Such opinions are often encountered in the Nordic newspapers these years. Justified or not, one can also turn the criticism upside down and develop new didactic tools exploiting the alledged impatience reconstrued as a capacity to communicate continuously.

This was our point of departure when we designed the interactive speech trainer Talebob (*Speech Bob*). Talebob is an internet-based language learning tool developed as an aid for Nordic pupils helping them train their spoken Danish with special regard to one of the most cumbersome aspects, the highly idiomatic pronunciation of certain phrases that occur in almost any informal conversation.

Many students of Danish report that, even though they have acquired what they believed to be a decent conduct of Danish, they nontheless feel helpless at their first encounter with the Danes habitually speaking very fast, in a style loaded with reductions, lenisions, assimilations and ligatures. Consider a few examples.

"d<u>e</u>t <u>e</u>r j<u>o</u> <u>i</u>kke n<u>o</u>get <u>a</u>t sn<u>a</u>kke <u>o</u>m"
(8 lexical syllables, full vowels <u>underlined</u>)

[dj<u>o</u>Jgn<u>å</u>D:sn<u>a</u>g<u>C</u>m][1]
(4 phonetic syllables, full vowels <u>underlined</u>)

This often heard phrase (literaly: *that is nothing to talk about*, meaning: *it's not a problem*) is routinely uttered in four phonetic syllables only, and with a highly predictable prosodic contour. If pronounced in accordance with the productive rules of Danish phonetics, reproducing *all* of the phonological vowels (as a typical rule-based TTS voice does), this phrase would probably be perceived by the native Dane as a composition of several independent semanitic units in various relations, a speech act (*snakke om*), a predicative modifier (*jo*), and a negated quantifier (*ikke noget*), in short, a fully fledged proposition to be compositionally evaluated.

Consider an other example, "tak skal du have" (literally: *thanks shall you have,* meaning: *thank you*), along with its highly idiomatic pronunciation patterns.

[t'Agsgaduh,a:?]	unmarked-polite, mildly grateful
[t'Agsgaduha]	impressed (no gratitude involved)
[tAgsgad'uh,a:?]	repulsed, sullen (anti-grateful)

[1]Here (and in the following) phonetic renderings are shown in SAMPA compliant format, cf. http://www.phon.ucl.ac.uk/home/sampa/danish.htm

Peter Juel Henrichsen 2015. Taking the Danish Speech Trainer from CALL to ICALL. *Proceedings of the 4th workshop on NLP for Computer Assisted Language Learning at NODALIDA 2015.* NEALT Proceedings Series 26 / Linköping Electronic Conference Proceedings 114: 11–20.

Many Greenlandic, Faroese, and Icelanding children report the Danes to be unexpectedly difficult to understand at their first encounter, even after several years of Danish studies, especially because the informal phrases occur so frequently. Unfortunately, West-Nordic teachers of Danish report that no teaching materials are available training this particular aspect of spoken Danish.

Talebob is meant as a remedy. It is conceived and designed by Danish computational linguists in cooperation with Icelandic researchers in didactics and West-Nordic school teachers. Talebob (ver. 1) is currently being tested in public schools in Nuuk, Hafnarfjörður and Tórshavn. Early experiments are also being carried out in Denmark with adult L2-learners.

Talebob was designed to help language students (9+ years of age) practice the pronunciation of such frequent phrases, often rich in function words (pronouns, connectives, adverbs and prepositions). As mentioned, their pronunciation patterns are typically highly conventionalized and are often in conflict with the general and productive rules of Danish pronunciation.

In the following, we first present Talebob in its current version and then reflect on how to develop the tool further. Sections 2-5 cover the technological and linguistic aspects of Talebob's design (front-end, back-end, and system architecture). In section 6 we reflect on various linguistic aspects of Talebob, in current and future versions. We conclude in section 7 with some remarks on Talebob (and interactive language learning tools in general) as an approach to screening large populations of pupils.

Example phrases are quoted in Danish and (being highly idiomatic) translated only when necessary.

2 Talebob as a CALL tool

Talebob is a tool for computer-assisted language learning (CALL), and it can be seen as a technically updated continuation of the classic language lab. Many readers will probably remember from their school days the setup with study booths equipped with a cassette deck for recording and playback, enabling oral communication with the language teacher on a one-to-one basis. The language lab (e.g. Thorborg 2003, 2006) stimulated the pupil's spoken language production and in this respect was a huge improvement over L2 exercises based on rehearsed dialogues. Of course the attention from the teacher was a scarce resource, and each pupil could not expect more than a few minutes of personal instruction during a lesson.

One of our main goals with Talebob is to take the language lab a step further towards interactivity such that each language production will yield an informed comment, either an appreciation or a constructive correction. In other words, Talebob should give the pupil a feeling of being heard.

3 Talebob's front-end

School children are used to computer games with a visual side approaching virtual reality. Rather than competing on graphics we wanted to attract our users through a carefully designed interactivity offering meaningful replies on all contacts. Talebob should thus behave as an attentive listener and competent evaluator.

The Talebob challenge consists of 30 tasks, each focused on a specific Danish phrase such as greeting formulae (*godmorgen*), common requests (*gi'r du en kop kaffe?*), and emotional expressions (*er du rigtig klog?!*). Common to such phrases is that their communicative effects may change radically with the smallest twists of the pronunciation. An inconspicuously looking phrase like "tak skal du have" (*thank you*) may be perceived as being ironic, impressed, tired, cordial, hateful, or just plainly informative depending on subtle prosodic modifications (e.g. changing the relative weight of the main stresses slightly). Being able to control such details is an intrinsic part of one's L1 competence, but is often difficult for L2 learners to acquire. Talebob allows the pupil to repeat each phrase as many times as needed, informed by Talebob's feedback. The phrase prompts are produced by a native speaker aiming for an 'ecological' pronunciation that no Dane would object to.

For each Talebob-task the pupil

1. selects a phrase,
2. listens to the phrase prompt (using the Lyt-Til-Frasen button),
3. reproduces the prompt orally (using Optag/Stop buttons for recording), mimicking it closely wrt. articulation, prosody, and tempo,
4. compares prompt and own production auditorily (pressing Lyt-Til-Optagelsen),
5. repeats steps 2-4 until entirely satisfied, then presses Send for evaluation,
6. consults the returned Talebob comment (either a success message sending the pupil to the next task, or a try-again advising the pupil how to improve)

Pressing Send invokes the Talebob acoustic analyzer, returning a smiley, either happy, neutral, or sad. With a happy smiley **:-)** the pupil has completed the task and may continue with the next phrase. Level-1 is done when the first five tasks are completed, level-2 has ten tasks, and level-3 fifteen. The phrases are ordered progressively, from single words and simple phrases in level-1 (*godmorgen, værsgo!*), frequent idioms in level-2 (*hvordan går det?*, *tak i lige måde*), to more expressive phrases in level-3 (*det siger du ikke?*, *hellere end gerne!*). When all tasks in level-3 are done, the Talebob challenge is passed.

Talebob's front-end is illustrated in fig. 1-3.

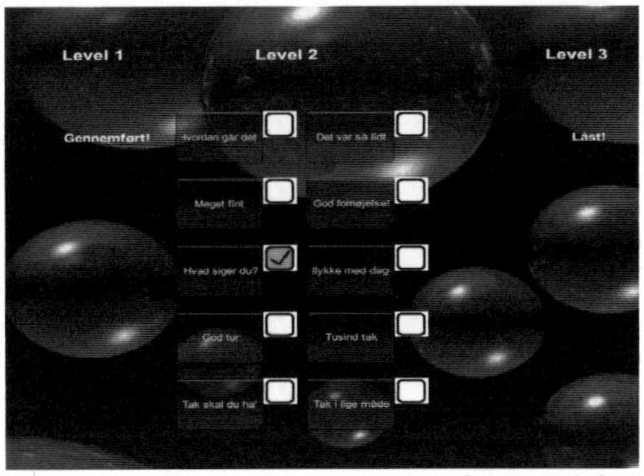

Figure 1. Screenshot (excerpt) from Talebob task-page, level 2, with one phrase passed.

Figure 2. Screenshot (excerpt) from Talebob return-page, level 2, not-passed.

Figure 3. Screenshot (excerpt) from Talebob return-page, level 2, passed.

4 Talebob's back-end (acoustic analysis)

The two sound files submitted (with the Send button) are evaluated in the Talebob back-end application. The acoustic analysis compares the prompt version (P) and the user's own production (U) sampling both files for F0 (pitch in Hz) and INT (intensity in dB), being unanimously considered as the most relevant parameters for acoustic-phonetic evaluation, both relating directly to phonetically features like stress, tone, sonority, occlusion, etc.[2] The linguistic evaluation is focused on the concordance of P

[2] F0 and INT are measured using the Praat toolkit (www.fon.hum.uva.nl/praat), window size 5 ms, filter settings = *Pitch (ac)... 0.005 75 15 yes 0.03 0.45 0.01 0.4 0.14 600; Intensity... 75 0.005 yes.* We also experimented with HNR (harmonicity-to-noise ratio) and various spectral filterings, but found them to be too noise sensitive. Classrooms are not quiet places!

and U wrt. speech tempo, global prosody, and articulation.

The speech tempo factor (*STF*) is determined as the ratio of durations for P and U,

$$STF = \text{duration(P)} : \text{duration(U)}$$

STF is calculated from INT data. First the zero level for INT in U is estimated, corresponding to 'no speech' in the given signal (this calibration can be tricky, especially for noise-prone samples, and is always a matter of heuristics). Then the zero level (0 dB after calibration) is used to delimit the speech production in U. By definition the optimum value for *STF* is 1.0, and productions approaching this value will trigger the comment "Meget fint taletempo" (*excellent speech tempo*). Lesser or greater values return instructions to speak faster or slower, respectively.

Prosody and articulation analyses are based on F0 measurements. Only the sonorant parts of P and U are sampled - that is, the segments of the speech signals where a pitch value can be meaningfully estimated, thus excluding obstruent sounds and moments of silence (e.g. between words). All frequency data are stored as logarithmic values (more convenient for statistical use). Many of Talebob's users are children, and their speech productions will often be higher-pitched than the phrase prompt on average. This global difference in pitch is of course irrelevant to the Talebob evaluation, so the F0 dataset for U is normalized (each sample multiplied with a derived constant) equalizing the average pitch of U and P.

After these preparatory steps, the prosodic evaluation is done. The calculation is based on 10 qualified datapoints for each (normalized) dataset U and P, in a procedure best explained by an example. Say 130 valid pitch samples were derived from P; the first datapoint for P (call it $f_{1,P}$) is then derived as the mean value for the first 13 samples; the 2nd datapoint ($f_{2,P}$) for samples 14..26, et cetera, up to ($f_{10,P}$) and ($f_{10,U}$). Finally the prosodic deviation (*ProsDev*) of U wrt. P is calculated by summation of 'errors',

$$ProsDev = |f_{1,P}-f_{1,S}| + |f_{2,P}-f_{2,S}| + .. + |f_{10,P}-f_{10,S}|$$

This particular *ProsDev* formula was designed to meet two special requirements. Firstly it abstracts away any temporal incongruities between U and P (already addressed by the *STF* score); secondly it copes well with the unpredictable number of valid F0 samples for U (sometimes as few as 15-20 for short speech productions in noisy surroundings, while P may produce 3-4 times more), preserving commensurability. For low *ProsErr* values, Talebob returns a praising comment "Dit tonefald er fint", and otherwise an instruction how to improve, e.g. "Prøv at tale mere livligt" (*try speaking more lively*).

The articulation is evaluated (*ArtEval*) along the same lines, but focusing on local incongruities rather than the phrase as a whole. First 30 qualified datapoints are derived following the procedure above, using numerical interpolation if necessitated by data sparseness. Error analyses (calculated as for *ProsDev*, mutatis mutandis) are done for datapoints 1..10, 11..20, and 21..30,

$$ArtEval(a,b) = \sum_{n=a}^{b} \left(F_{n,P} - F_{n,U}\right),$$

F being is the 30-point dataset (otherwise as *f* above). The results for *ArtEval*(1,10), *ArtEval*(11,20), and *ArtEval*(21,30) represents the first, middle, and last part of the utterance as reflected in the returned comments: "Prøv at tale tydeligere i de første/midterste/sidste ord" (*try to speak more clearly in the first/middle/final words*), a somewhat vague instruction perhaps, but faced with the impatience and limited vocabulary of pupils we had to prioritize didactive effect over descriptive accuracy.

Summing up, feedback from Talebob consists in three comments, one for each of the evaluation criteria (tempo, prosody, and pronunciation), and in addition a smiley representing the overall performance. The *happy* smiley ('task completed') is given when each of the three evaluation results has met a (pre-set) acceptable limit, the *sad* smiley is given if none of the limits are met, and the *medium* smiley otherwise.

See the discussion below on the linguistic relevance and scientific testability of the Talebob acoustic-phonetic design.

4.1 An example - phrase "hej med dig"

The graphs in fig. 4 and 5 both cover the phrase *hej med dig* in three speech productions, (*i*) the prompt, (*ii*) an Islandic pupil (boy, 7th grade) on 2nd attempt, and (*iii*) same pupil on 5th attempt. Notice that INT graphs are continuous, intensity being defined everywhere, while F0 graphs are interruped at unvoiced passages (e.g. the stopped [d] in *dig*).

The huge difference in speech tempo between 2nd and 5th attempt is easily appreciated in fig. 4. The very slow tempo in #2 (2nd attempt) triggered the Talebob comment "Du taler alt for langsomt" (*you speak much too slowly*); the pupil sped up and - as seen - eventually matched the prompt's tempo in #5. His pronunciation had also become more fluent, without the unwarranted separation of *hej* and *med* (cf. the INT dip around *t*=0.45" in the #2 graph, absent from both #5 and the prompt). Concerning the prosodic contour, notice that the F0 envelope for #2 and #5 (cf. fig. 5) both match the prompt quite closely when abstracting away from the different tempi: two stable pitch inclinations with an intervening resetting, corresponding to the two stress groups in the (most common) Danish pronunciation. Consequently, *ProsDev* is relatively low in both cases, having Talebob praise the pronunciation in both cases: "Meget fint tonefald" (*very good tone-of-voice*). At the same time, though, the *ArtEval*-based analysis shows a 'lack' of pitch modulation in #2 (preceived as mumbling, and producing a relatively poor *ArtEval* value), in this case triggering the comment for #2: "Prøv at tale tydeligere" (*try to pronounce the words more clearly*). Through his next attempts, the pupil improved his pronunciation gradually, and by #5, the *ArtEval* value passed the accept limit, allowing Talebob to issue a happy smiley (notice though in fig. 5 that the pitch range is still somewhat limited for #5).

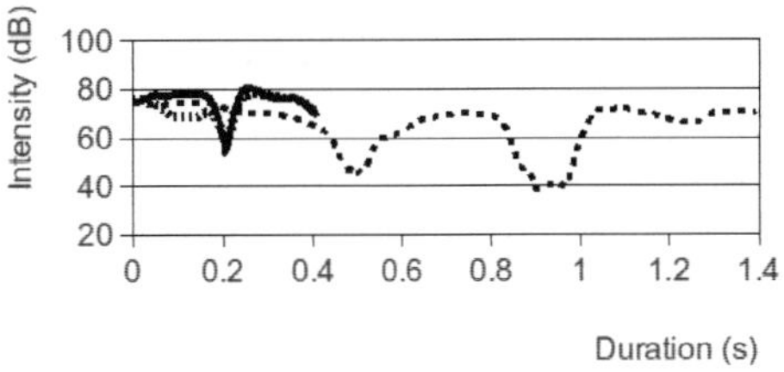

Figure 4. Phrase "hej med dig", intensity data; prompt (solid line), Icelandic pupil's 2nd/5th attempt (dispersed/close dots)

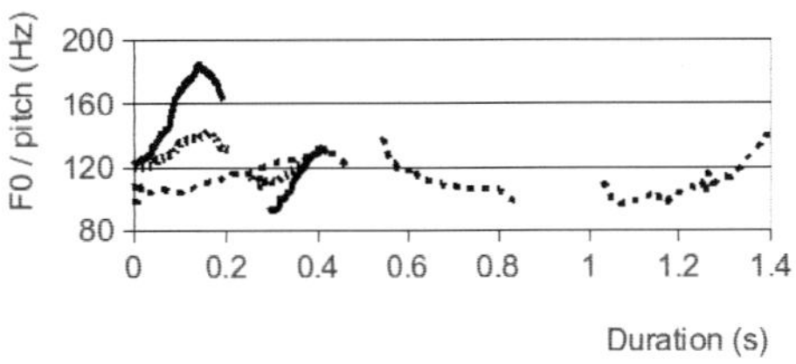

Figure 5. Phrase "hej med dig", pitch data; prompt (solid line), Icelandic pupil's 2nd/5th attempt (dispersed/close dots)

5 System architecture

The Talebob development had three phases. First an appropriate set of phrases was selected and recorded, largely recycling materials and selection criteria from earlier CALL projects including Allwood et al (2005), Selsøe et al (2004), Henrichsen (2004, 2004b, 2014). Then the back-end was programmed and tested (main programs written in Perl using the standard open-source modules only, enhanced with Unix system calls). The front-end, however, presented us with an unexpected challenge. Nobody could update us on the IT situation in West-Nordic schools, neither for hardware, software, operating system, local IT-assistance, or even internet connectivity. Yet we did not want any potential user to go down on equipment. Also we did not want to preclude any working places. Some pupils prefer to train in the privacy of their home while others like to share. We did not want to force any limitations on the user on purely technical grounds. This led us to consider three front-end/back-end architectures (presented as *A1*, *A2*, and *A3*).

A1. Stand-alone (program installed on user's own hardware: pc, tablet, or smartphone)

PRO:

- Independent of internet connectivity
- Quick query-response cycle

CON:

- Programming/maintenance of back-end for a range of unknown hardware is demanding
- Technical support (from developer to pupil, teacher and/or local IT helpdesk) is hard due to physical and time-zone distance
- Monitoring of users' performance and progress is difficult
- System updates are hard to communicate

A2. Browser-based

PRO:

- Contacts between users and server can be logged (easier maintenance & development)
- Developers can make performance data available to teachers and others online
- Browser-based front-end using HTML5 and CSS is (fairly) hardware independent

CON:

- Stands or falls with user's connectivity
- 100% server uptime is mandatory
- HTML5 audio, especially for recording, is currently not fully supported in all browsers

A3. Internet-based, but dedicated front-end

The advantages are the same as for *A2*, and in addition the HTML5 problem can be avoided. Also we do not need to instruct users to download this or that internet-browser. The main hurdle being that users have to install a dedicated program prior to their first positive Talebob experience.

Even if *A2* seemed to us to be the best alternative overall, we settled on *A3* for practical reasons. Many potential users are Explorer fans and did not care to install a new browser with better HTML5 support, such as Chrome, Firefox, or even IE 9+.

As the developer team had some experience with Unity4 (www.unity4.com), in particular its strong audio support and graphics drivers, we settled for this programming workbench. Unity4 is freely available (in the open-source version) and so does not compromize Talebob as a shareable application. Unity4 programs compile to all common operating systems (even older versions) including Linux, Mac, Win, Android, etc. The flip side of the coin is that potential Talebob users have to download an executable (via Dropbox, as explained in the Taleboblen homepage, www.taleboblen.hi.is), unzip it, and invoke it using their own operating system. Simple as these procedures may be for skilled IT-users, they showed to be problematic for many language teachers and even local IT-helpdesks. We intend to launch a purely browser-based Talebob-version in the near future, as a supplement to the current version.

For an interesting discussion on CALL design principles for tools training spoken language, see Appel et al (2012). González (2012) and Mbah et al (2013) have experimented with minimalistic CALL applications for English teaching.

6 Linguistic reflections

In our paper accepted for presentation at the NODALIDA 2015 main session we report on our practical evaluations of Talebob as a didactic tool: How we evaluated the soundness and relevance of the linguistic feedback returned by the Talebob backend, and how Talebob was received by the pupils in the three regions (Greenland, Iceland, and the Faroes). Some preliminary quantitative results are also presented.

6.1 Talebob as a scientific enterprise

Our current evaluation scheme (based on *STF*, *ProsDev*, and *ArtEval*) has worked well, providing a useful compromise between linguistic precision and communicable (age-appropriate) advise. However, we are aware that this particular setup has not proved itself in a strict scientific sense. Maybe different formulae or new scoring procedures would allow even more useful feedback from Talebob. For example, we suspect that *ProsDev* and *ArtEval* definitions based on standard deviation rather than numerical distance may allow more specific corrections. New batteries of formulae are constantly being tested - still without this being driven by ideal linguistic criteria, but rather as a pragmatic and feedback-informed activity.

Actually, it's not clear to us that an 'ideal' configuration could be obtained at all. The most effective evaluation procedures, from a didactic point of view, would not rely solely on ideal linguistic criteria, but include the personal profiles of the pupils (degree of motivation, prior knowledge of Danish, own first language, general IT-experience, and more).

6.2 From CALL to ICALL

Having described the actual features and functions of Talebob in its present form, the following sections are more speculative. We wish to invite a discussion of three potential developments: how to enhance the feeling of naturalness and relevance to the speech productions; how to plan the portation of Talebob to other L2 scenaria; and how to exploit ICALL tools in general (Talebob being an example) for screening larger populations of L2 learning pupils.

6.3 Productive expressivity

Talebob is, of course, a low-knowledge system with very little in-built language competence. Inspired by the special focus of NLP4CALL we reflect upon how to induce an amount of linguistic 'intelligence' in Talebob without compromising the low-knowledge style tenet (we'll return to this point shortly).

After having passed level 3, users should feel comfortable with the Talebob feedback cycle. The new prosodic awareness could be developed further by having the user engage in a 'real' dialogue, exploring a kind of interactivity where the choice and production of a phrase (as opposed to another realization of the same lexical word sequence) have direct consequences for the continuation of the game (and score!).

By way of illustration, consider again the phrase *tak skal du have* repeated here for convenience.

p1.	[t'Agsgaduh,a:?]	polite, mildly grateful
p2.	[t'Agsgaduha]	impressed, shocked
p3.	[tAgsgad'uh,a:?]	repulsed, sullen

As opposed to the game levels 1-3, Talebob now takes the initative presenting an assertion among a1-a3 (randomly chosen).

a1:- her er din kaffe
(your coffee, here you are)
a2:- jeg har lige set en trafikulykke
(I just witnessed a traffic accident)
a3:- du skal da bare betale den ødelagte dør
(why don't you just pay for that broken door)

The user responds to the assertion by selecting one of the prosodic renderings P1-P3 of the target phrase and then uploads his speech production.

Talebob performs an acoustic comparison between the user input and the canned versions, deciding the closest match and, hence, how to continue the conversation in a coherent manner.

Coherent discourse

T:- her er din kaffe (*here is your coffee*)
U:- tak skal du ha' [neutral-polite, mildly grateful]

T_a:- bruger du mælk og sukker? (*milk or suger?*)
or
T_b:- var der andet? (*you want anything else?*)

Anomalous user input

T:- her er din kaffe (*here is your coffee*)
U*:- tak *SKAL* du ha'! [impressed/chocked]

T^*_a:- er der noget galt? [is *something wrong?*]
or
T^*_b:- gør du nar af mig? [*are you making fun?*]

Likewise for the other predictable dialogue paths. Probably only a subset of the phrases included in the current Talebob will be suitable for this new "stimulus-response" scheme, calling for new selection criteria in the compilation of the phrasicon (phrase selection). Single- and multi-word interjections ('ja', 'nej', 'nå'[3], 'okay', 'klart', 'hold kæft', 'er det sandt?', etc) immediately spring to mind. As a side-effect of this construction work, we -- the linguists -- will probably also learn our own language better!

We consider using TTS for presenting the priming assertions, adding still more realism to the dialogue training. We will need a synthetic voice giving us full prosodic control. For this reason we opt for a diphone voice, since the (more modern) unit-selection based voices typically achieve their naturalness by sacrificing the prosodic control of the output. The TTS can be tried at http://lab.homunculus.dk/Talebob. With the TTS-enhancement, one could have even the priming assertion itself change its triggering potential (i.e. the adequate response) as a function of it's prosodic contour alone.

6.4 A portation tool kit

There is nothing intrinsically 'Danish' about Talebob; the acoustic analysis and scoring procedures have no language-specific parts. Indeed, any user utterance with a pitch envelope similar to the reference utterance would achieve a high score, regardless of the lexical content of the utterance. This can be seen as a strength or a weakness in a broader NLP perspective, and indeed our academic discussion partners have expressed a wide range of opinions about this. Suffice it to say that we have not, until now, encoutered any 'cheating' among pupil users, rather the opposite: judging from our own evaluation of the recorded sound productions, all pupil users without exception appear to have worked on improving not only their prosodic performance (which is monitored by Talebob), but also their phonetic accuracy (which is not). This benign placebo effect is, in our view, an important observation in its own right, sharing in effect the evaluation burden between the CALL tool (which can never compete with a professional language teacher anyway) and the learner himself (who may not even be aware of his self-monitoring). In order to quantify the placebo effects, we would need to perform a controlled experiment with two user groups, one using a mock-version of Talebob producing random feedback, and one control group using Talebob as is. We have not performed such an experiment, but it might be an interesting one.

As said, the value of low- or no-knowledge CALL tools is a controversial issue. However, in one respect, Talebob's linguistic ignorance is an undisputable advantage. When porting Talebob to new L2 teaching scenaria, hardly any software modifications will be needed, only an editorial process of selecting 30 (or more) suitable phrases followed by a recording session with one or more native speakers with a flair for 'ecological pronunciation'. The technical integration of these materials is fairly trivial (though some languages may require slight changes in the acoustic setup). In this respect, Talebob's simplistic speech evaluation differs from the technologically far more sophisticated CALL tools for L2 conversational training available in the market, such as Cooori (www.cooori.com), Wang (2011), de Vries (2014), and Mirzaei et al (2014), all including a fully-fledged ASR component (automatic speech recognition).

We are currently taking the first steps towards a tool kit allowing any L2 teacher, perhaps with some general IT experience, to compile a localized Talebob version for use in his own classroom. As illustrated in figure 6 below, the necessary activities are concentrated on (i) compiling the phrasicon (based on a manual of selection criteria), (ii) producing the speech prompts (in accordance with certain pronunciation principles), (iii) adjusting the Commentary (the repertoire of eventual feed-back messages), (iv) generating the two essential executives (the front-end and back-end), (v) installing the *BE* (back-end application) on one's local web-server and, finally (vi) distributing the *FE* (front-end aplication) to the pupils or other end-users.

---

[3] The many semantic facets of the Danish interjection 'nå' [n'C] is ingeniously protraited in the famous song, by Poul Henningsen

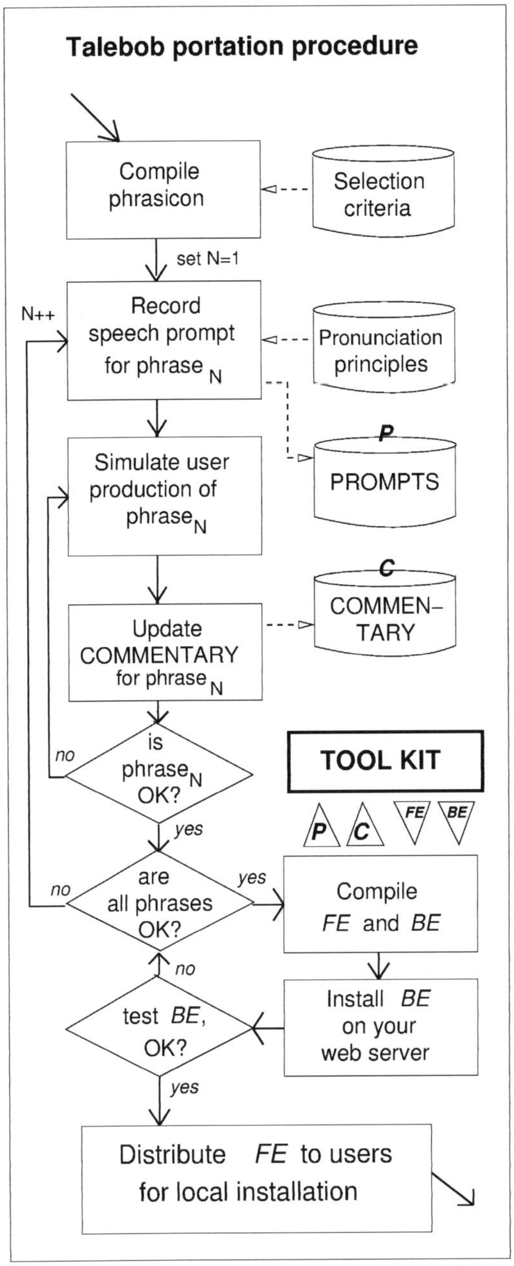

Figure 6. Using the Talebob Portation Tool Kit.

6.5 ICALL-based monitoring

In this concluding section we touch on ICALL tools for societal use in a broader perspective (with Talebob as an example) as a means of gathering data not only relevant to didactic practices and research, but to basic linguistic research as well, and even (potentially) to political bodies, providing them with quantitative data for longitudinal studies of larger populations of students.

Until now we have mainly tested Talebob as a didactic tool to enhance the spoken language teaching in a classroom setting. However, as we do log all user productions and shall continue doing so for new versions, Talebob is not only useful as a didactic tool, but as a generator of substantial amounts of experimental data of a linguistic data type that can otherwise be difficult to elicit, exhibiting the pronunciation patterns of L2 learners in great detail. To our knowledge, no-one has produced a quantitatively based comparative study of the pronunciation patterns of Danish students. We are currently compiling data for such a paper, charting the pronunciation habits (and skills) as a function of their own first language, their prior exposure to Danish, their gender and age, self-declared degree of motivation, etc.

We thus wish to point to Talebob as an example of CALL-based screening of large groups of pupils. Access to statistical information about the progress of individual pupils, classes, and even populations of classes may be useful even for political decision-makers. Such considerations are highly relevant in Denmark right now, the 2014 school reform currently being implemented. For the first time ever English is now taught from first grade in Denmark. Spokesmen for the teachers are constantly expressing concerns about the lack of training programmes for teachers new to the challenge of teaching English to minors. Objective means for assessing the learning patterns are frequently called for in the press and in parliament. We believe that cleverly designed CALL-tools could play a decisive role in this debate.

We are preparing a Talebob version adapted for English phrases, planning experiments with first graders during 2015 hopefully laying the ground for a longitudinal study. We do hope that Nordic researchers and Danish politicians will pick up on this unique historical opportunity.

7 A concluding remark

After having tested Talebob extensively for almost six months now with L2 learners of Danish in three countries, our most significant overall opservation is that pupil users generally *like* Talebob and spend far more time (at home and in school) training Danish pronunciation than ever before (Hauksdottir and Henrichsen (in prep.)). We have not yet performed any quantitative evaluations of the didactic effects, so we do not know whether Talebob can actually teach pupils a better Danish. Nevertheless, teachers in our test group (especially Icelanders) report that most of their pupils never practiced spoken Danish before unless forced. A majority of pupils report that they feel more confident now when using Danish speech productively (Hauksdottir and Henrichsen (in prep.)). This result alone, we feel, have made Talebob a worthwhile enterprise.

Acknowledgments

The presented work is a part of the ongoing Nordic project "Talehjælp til Dansk som Nabosprog" 2013-2015, supported by NorFA and Nordisk Ministerråd/Nordplus. We gratefully acknowledge their contributions. The project combines didactic and computational-linguistic research in Iceland, Denmark, and Sweden with practical implementation work by language teachers in Nuuk, Hafnarfjörður and Tórshavn (visit http://www.taleboblen.hi.is). Many have thus contributed, from a geographical area spanning five time zones. One, however, outshines all others: project leader and initiator Auður Hauksdóttir. Thanks to Auður for her many years as a powerstation in Nordic L2 didactics.

References

de Vries, B. P., Cucchiarini, C., Bodnar, S.. 2014. *Automatic Feedback on Spoken Dutch of Low-Educated Learners: An ASR-based CALL study*. Proceed. of EUROCALL 2014 (to appear).

Mbah, E.E., Mhab, B.M., Iloene, M.I., Iloene, G.O. 2013. *Podcasts for Learning English Pronunciation in Igboland: Students' Experiences and Expectations*. EUROCALL 2013.

González, J.F. 2012. *Can Apple's iPhone Help to Improve English Pronunciation Autonomously? State of the App*. EUROCALL 2012

Appel, C., Robbins, J., Moré, J., Mullen, T. 2012. *Task and Tool Interface Design for L2 Speaking Interaction Online*. EUROCALL 2012

Hauksdottir, A., Henrichsen, P.J. (in prep.) *Danskfaget i Vestnorden og det Digitale Læremiddel Taleboblen*

Thorborg, L. 2006. *Dansk Udtale i 49 Tekster*. Synope, ISBN 87-91909-01-5 (cd and book)

Thorborg, L. 2003. *Dansk Udtale - Øvebog*. Synope, ISBN 87-988509-4-6 (cd and book)

Selsøe Sørensen, H., Henrichsen, P.J., Hansen, C. 2004. *NorFA CALL net: Nordisk Netværk om Computerstøttet Unvervisning i Nordiske Sprog*; Nordisk Sprogteknologisk Forskningsprogram 2000-2004, Samfundslitteratur Press, 224pp.

Wang, H., T. Kawahara and Y. Wang. 2011. *Improving Non-native Speech Recognition Performance by Discriminative Training for Language Model in a CALL System;* INTERSPEECH 2011, 27-31

Mirzaei (2014) *Partial and synchronized captioning: A new tool for second language listening development;* EUROCALL 2014.

Henrichsen, P.J. 2004. *The Twisted Tongue; Tools for Teaching Danish Pronunciation Using a Synthetic Voice*; in Henrichsen (2004b)

Henrichsen, P.J. 2004b. *"CALL for the Nordic Languages - tools and methods for Computer Assisted Language Learning;* Cph. Studies in Language 30/2004

Allwood, J. and Henrichsen, P.J. (eds). 2005. *SweDanes for CALL - A corpus and computer-based student's aid for comparison of Swedish and Danish spoken language.* NorFA CALL NET (cd with manual).

Using Shallow Syntactic Features to Measure Influences of L1 and Proficiency Level in EFL Writings

Andrea Horbach[⋆]**, Jonathan Poitz**[⋆]**, Alexis Palmer**[†]
[⋆] Department of Computational Linguistics, Saarland University, Saarbrücken, Germany
[†]Institute for Natural Language Processing, Stuttgart University, Stuttgart, Germany
[⋆](andrea|jpoitz)@coli.uni-saarland.de, [†]alexis.palmer@ims.uni-stuttgart.de

Abstract

This paper proposes a framework for modeling and analyzing differences between texts written by different subgroups of learners of English as a Foreign Language (organized according to native language (L1) and proficiency level). Using frequency vectors of both POS-trigrams and mixed POS and function word trigrams, we compare learner language variants both to each other and to native English, German, and Chinese texts. We introduce the *trigram usage factor* metric for identifying sequences that are especially characteristic of a particular subgroup of learners. We show that distance between learner English and native English decreases with proficiency. Next we compare the distance between learner English and other native languages. Finally, we show that automatic proficiency classification benefits from using L1-specific classifiers.

1 Introduction

When learning to write in a foreign language (L2), learners tend to make some errors that arise via the transfer of properties of their native language (L1). In other words, sometimes lexical, syntactic, semantic, or pragmatic characteristics of a learner's L1 arise in L2 writing in ways that are either wrong or simply not typical for native speaker writers. We build on the notion of Selinker (Selinker, 1972), who introduced the concept of *interlanguage*, the specific language systems of individual language learners. A learner's interlanguage includes, among other influences, features of the learner's L1, and speakers of the same L1 often develop similar interlanguages.

In this paper, we propose a new way of modeling learner language that allows us to compare L2 texts produced by learners with various L1s both to each other and to texts written by native speakers of various languages. We investigate, via several different exploratory studies, the role of L1 influences on the shallow syntactic structures produced by learners of English as a Foreign Language (EFL).

Our shallow syntactic analysis consists of part-of-speech (POS) tags and certain lexical items, primarily closed-class function words. In this way we abstract away (to a large extent) from lexical biases due to topic, and instead focus on syntactic aspects of the learner language. This approach has also been used in work on Native Language Identification (Nagata and Whittaker, 2013; Wong et al., 2012). We build a vector space of trigram frequencies for different groups of learners of English, as well as for native speakers of several languages, and we use these vectors to compare language variants, using one standard similarity metric and one novel similarity metric. The models are described in more detail in Sec. 4.

The first aim of the study is to confirm the validity of this modeling approach in the language learning context (Sec. 5.1). Our model shows (not surprisingly) that native English and L2 English indeed differ in the distribution of our vector components: learners of English use structures with different frequencies than native speakers. A key finding here is that the distance between native English and L2 English, measured by distributional similarity in the trigram vector space, decreases as learners become more proficient, showing the validity of our model.

We further investigate how these deviations vary across different L1s, identifying certain patterns of deviation that can be linked to syntactic properties of the L1 (Sec. 5.2). Here we introduce our *trigram usage factor* metric, which allows us to identify particular trigrams which are either over- or underused by a particular group of

Andrea Horbach, Jonathan Poitz and Alexis Palmer 2015. Using shallow syntactic features to measure influences of L1 and proficiency level in EFL writings. *Proceedings of the 4th workshop on NLP for Computer Assisted Language Learning at NODALIDA 2015*. NEALT Proceedings Series 26 / Linköping Electronic Conference Proceedings 114: 21–34.

learners. Brief case studies for English written by speakers of German, Japanese, Turkish, and French show that our model picks up interesting L1-specific properties. We further find that instances of overused trigrams often represent stylistic differences rather than actual errors, and only in certain selected contexts can the usage factor help to automatically identify problematic constructions in learner text.

Next, we consider how the influence of students' L1 changes as learners become more proficient in the relevant L2, in this case English (Sec. 5.3). We investigate this by measuring the similarity between various English learner groups and texts written by native speakers of English, German, and Chinese.

This investigation requires mapping the POS tags for English, German, and Chinese into the Universal Tagset (Petrov et al., 2012), a coarse-grained tagset designed to be suitable for all languages (as the name suggests). We use existing mapping scripts to convert tagsets for the three languages into the Universal Tagset, and we build a new vector space based on the coarse-grained POS tags. In every case, even low-proficiency L2-English is closer to native English than to either native German or native Chinese. Some effects seem to be due at least in part to typological differences between L1s.

Finally, building on the observation that trigram distributions change as learner proficiency increases, we use trigram vectors as features for a simple learner-proficiency classifier (Sec. 5.4). The results of this very preliminary study are mixed: though the features are not able to beat a simple baseline, we do show that the accuracy of proficiency classification improves when we classify groups of essays written by learners with a shared L1. In other words, the changes in trigram distributions according to proficiency are at least to some extent influenced by the native language of the learner.

2 Related Work

Aspects of our approach are similar to some work in grammatical error detection that also makes use of trigrams or similar measures. For example, the ALEC system (Chodorow and Leacock, 2000) compares the local context of a specific word in an essay to the context in a native corpus to identify erroneous usages in learner texts.

Tetreault and Chodorow (2009) use region specific web counts to identify linguistic phenomena on the lexical level that are particularly problematic for a certain geographic region, i.e. speakers of a certain L1. They compare how often a certain construction that can be indicative of an error is used in comparison to its correct counterpart in that region and compare this ratio to the one in a native population. In this way, they reliably detect constructions corresponding to common errors for learners of that L1. The approach to model learner language for multiple individual L1s is not commonly integrated into Automatic Error Detection, but used also in some other works such as (Hermet and Désilets, 2009).

Sun et al. (2007) use so-called labeled sequential patterns that overcome the locality of trigrams and consist of (not necessarily consecutive) sequences of words that might be indicative of errors. They mine such patterns and use them to classify correct and erroneous sentences.

While these approaches mostly focus on lexical items and errors connected to them, we stay with our analyses on the side of POS and mixed model trigrams. In terms of error detection, we thus lack the granularity needed for this task and rather observe over- and underusages that might be indicative of errors but do not directly allow error classification. However, for the goal of comparing different language learner variants as a whole to native English, we obtain models that avoid data sparseness and filter out most of the topic bias present in lexical models.

3 Data and Preprocessing

This section describes the four corpora used in our experiments and preprocessing steps. The primary corpus is the ETS Corpus of Non-Native Written English, which contains essays in English from learners from eleven different L1s. The secondary resources used are three corpora of texts written by native speakers: LOCNESS for English, the FalkoEssayL1 corpus for German, and the Penn Chinese Treebank for Chinese.

3.1 Corpora

The ETS Corpus of Non-Native Written English. The ETS corpus (Blanchard et al., 2014) contains a total of 12,100 essays (more than 4 million tokens) from EFL learners of eleven different L1 origins, namely Arabic, Chinese, French, Ger-

	low		medium		high	
Arabic (ARA)	66146	(296)	197217	(605)	77234	(199)
German (DEU)	3711	(15)	142380	(412)	268309	(673)
French (FRA)	13839	(63)	195455	(577)	181202	(460)
Hindi (HIN)	8670	(29)	151265	(429)	263322	(642)
Italian (ITA)	37307	(164)	201745	(623)	117699	(313)
Japanese (JPN)	46451	(233)	220426	(679)	75236	(188)
Korean (KOR)	35754	(169)	228526	(678)	106199	(253)
Spanish (SPA)	19904	(79)	192858	(563)	184641	(458)
Telugu (TEL)	27968	(94)	229723	(659)	139085	(347)
Turkish (TUR)	19636	(90)	208241	(616)	158060	(394)
Chinese (ZHO)	24661	(98)	258462	(727)	114992	(275)

Table 1: Number of tokens (and essays) per language and proficiency

man, Hindi, Italian, Japanese, Korean, Spanish, Telugu and Turkish. The dataset is composed of responses in the TOEFL test to 8 different prompts and is mainly used for native language identification tasks. It is thus balanced over languages, i.e. 1100 essays per language. The essays also come with proficiency information on three levels (*low*, *medium* and *high*). Table 1 shows the distribution over languages and proficiency levels. We can see that the levels are not balanced and we have substantially more essays from a medium proficiency range than for low or high proficiency.

Proficiency levels are derived from 5-point essay scores assigned by human raters, who adressed various aspects of an essay in their grade, such as lexical choice, grammar, coherence and argumentative structure.

The LOCNESS corpus. The LOCNESS corpus[1] contains 410 essays from British and American high school students, amounting to 320,000 tokens of text. We use it as a comparison corpus for comparing the different variants of L2 writings to native English of the same text type, i.e. argumentative essays.

The Falko-L1 corpus. The FalkoEssayL1 corpus (Reznicek et al., 2012) is a corpus of native German argumentative essays written by students in response to four different prompts. It contains 95 texts with a total of approximately 70,000 tokens. The texts have been error-annotated and normalized. We use in our experiments the so-called target hypothesis *ZH1* that has the goal of correcting primarily orthographical and morphosyntactic errors. This version of the corpus is chosen over the raw essay texts in order to minimize POS tagging problems due to misspelled and therefore unknown words.

The Penn Chinese Treebank. The Penn Chinese Treebank (Xue et al., 2002) is a corpus of Chinese news texts that comes already with - among other annotation layers - manual annotations for word segmentation and POS tags.

3.2 Preprocessing

The ETS corpus is already tokenized, and we use this tokenization. Falko and Penn Chinese Treebank come with token and POS annotations. LOCNESS requires sentence-splitting and tokenization, for which we use the OpenNLP toolkit.[2] The final step needed to have suitable input for our models is POS tagging. We use Treetagger (Schmid, 1994), which uses a refined form of the Penn Treebank tagset (Marcus et al., 1993), to tag all English texts. For a description of these tags, refer to Table 2. The other two corpora are pretagged, and in both cases we use the existing POS tags. Falko corpus texts (as well as the normalized form we use) have been tagged with the Treetagger and the STTS tagset (Schiller et al., 1999), and the Penn Chinese Treebank comes with manual POS annotations.

4 Models

The core of our modeling approach are trigrams in learner essays. N-gram features have proven useful in many natural language processing applications, including those aiming to capture differences between non-native texts written by learners

[1] https://www.uclouvain.be/en-cecl-locness.html

[2] https://opennlp.apache.org/

POS Tag	Meaning	POS Tag	Meaning
#	”#” character	RBR	adverb, comparative
$	currency symbol	RBS	adverb, superlative
“	opening quotes	RP	particle
”	closing quotes	SENT	end punctuation
(	opening braces (”(” or ”{”)	SYM	symbol
)	closing braces (”)” or ”}”)	TO	”to”
,	”,” character	UH	interjection
:	general joiner	VB	verb be, base form
CC	coordinating conjunction	VBD	verb be, past
CD	cardinal number	VBG	verb be, gerund/participle
DT	determiner	VBN	verb be, past participle
EX	existential there	VBP	verb be, pres non-3rd p.
FW	foreign word	VBZ	verb be, pres, 3rd p. sing
IN	preposition/subord. conj.	VH	verb have, base form
IN/that	complementizer	VHD	verb have, past
JJ	adjective	VHG	verb have, gerund/participle
JJR	adjective, comparative	VHN	verb have, past participle
JJS	adjective, superlative	VHP	verb have, pres non-3rd per.
LS	list marker	VHZ	verb have, pres 3rd per.sing
MD	modal	VV	verb, base form
NN	noun, singular or mass	VVD	verb, past tense
NNS	noun plural	VVG	verb, gerund/participle
NP	proper noun, singular	VVN	verb, past participle
NPS	proper noun, plural	VVP	verb, present, non-3rd p.
NS	–	VVZ	verb, present 3d p. sing.
PDT	predeterminer	WDT	wh-determiner
POS	possessive ending	WP	wh-pronoun
PP	personal pronoun	WP$	possessive wh-pronoun
PP$	possessive pronoun	WRB	wh-abverb
RB	adverb		

Table 2: Tags used for POS-tagging English content: the Treetagger version of the Penn Treebank tagset

with different L1s. One prominent example is native language identification where many systems use some sort of n-gram features (Tetreault et al., 2013). In our case, we use trigram models to capture syntactic properties of various subgroups of language learners, grouping by both L1 and proficiency level. We concentrate on trigrams as they are long enough to capture some context of a word, but do not cause sparse data problems.

We build a model of each particular learner group – for example, medium-proficiency learners whose native language is Hindi – by collecting frequency counts for a selected set of trigrams (here, the most frequent trigrams in a native English corpus). Trigram counts are extracted from the set of English essays written by that group of learners. For most studies, we build one vector for each *subcorpus* (in this case, HIN_medium), where the vector components are frequency counts for the given trigrams. We then can think of a vector space which contains vectors for all learner sub-corpora, which we also use for comparison in parts of study 1 (Sec. 5.1). In the final study (Sec. 5.4), and also for part of study 1 (Sec. 5.1), we build one such vector per essay.

Two different types of trigrams are used to build these models (see below). In both approaches, we count only trigrams which occur within sentences, and use <SENT> to represent the start of the sentence.[3]

POS models. In the *POS models*, vectors are constructed by extracting trigram counts from POS-tagged texts. This means that each word is tagged, and the original lexical material of the text is discarded. The aim of using POS tag sequences is to abstract away from concrete topics in the data and rely as much as possible on the grammatical structures present in the text.

Mixed models. In the *mixed models*, vectors are constructed by extracting trigram counts from texts that have been transformed into a mix of POS tags and lexical items (as done similarly by Nagata and Whittaker (2013) and Wong et al. (2012)).

The motivation for our mixed models is that many learner deviations manifest on the lexico-syntactic level rather than purely on the POS level. In other words, it often matters not just whether a preposition is used, but which one, or not only whether an article is used at all, but whether it is definite or indefinite. Those differences are captured by our mixed model, while still filtering out content-bearing material.

For open-class words, like nouns, verbs, and adjectives, words are replaced by their POS tags. Function words and closed-class words such as prepositions and articles remain unchanged.[4] Adverbs (RB) are a special case: we differentiate between those that end in *-ly*, which we treat as open-class, and all other adverbs, which we treat as closed-class. While this simple distinction is correct in most cases, there is room to further refine this heuristic. For instance, the word *only* is both an adverb and ends in *-ly*, however it is not a content word. Also the categories RBR and RBS (comparative and superlative, respectively) are not completely clear-cut. RBR can be the part of speech for function words like *more, less*, but likewise for content words like *better, faster, stronger*, and similarly for the superlative RBS tag.

5 Explorations

Having established the modeling set-up and model variants, we now describe the various studies in which we use this modeling framework to investigate L1 influences and their relation to learner proficiency level.

The first two studies (Sec. 5.1 and Sec. 5.2) examine L1-specific correlates in L2 writings, showing that essays written by EFL learners show certain properties specific to their native language. Some of the deviations from native English seen in learner essays can be attributed to specific syntactic differences between the languages, while others are characteristic of learner language in general. The third study (Sec. 5.3) compares EFL learner essays to native-speaker essays in German and Chinese, and the final study (Sec. 5.4) makes a first attempt to use our modeling framework for automatic proficiency classification.

5.1 Study 1: Measuring the distance between native and non-native English

In this study we investigate how far away from native English different learner groups are (i.e. individual combinations of L1 and proficiency level),

[3] We only allow this as the first word in a trigram.

[4] More specifically, lexical items are replaced by their POS tags when those tags are any of the following (from the Penn Treebank tagset): FW, JJ, JJR, JJS, NN, NNS, NP, NPS, RBR, RBS, UH, VB, VBD, VBG, VBN, VBP, VBZ, VH, VHD, VHG, VHN, VHP, VHZ, VV, VVD, VVG, VVN, VVP, VVZ, NS and CD.

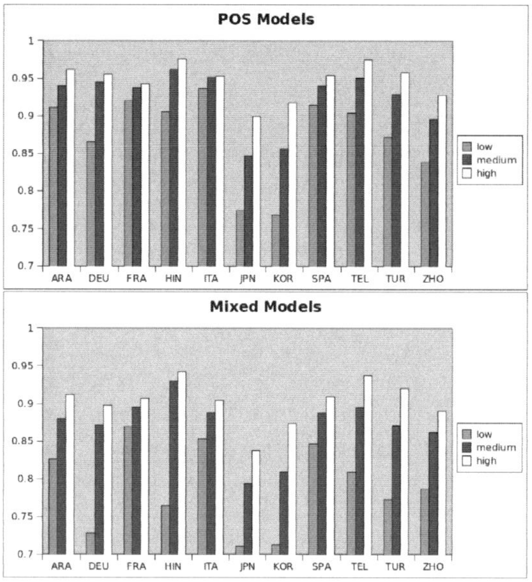

Figure 1: Cosine similarity between non-native English variants and native English, computed *per subcorpus*, for three different proficiency levels, using both POS trigrams (top) and mixed trigrams (bottom)

investigating differences both on the subcorpus level and on the essay level.

First, we model native English by building two feature vectors from the LOCNESS corpus, one with POS trigrams and one with mixed trigrams (see Sec. 4), each vector containing the 500 most frequent trigrams for that version of the corpus, with their raw frequency counts. Then, for each L1-proficiency subcorpus (i.e. for 33 subcorpora of the ETS corpus), we again build two feature vectors, each containing the absolute frequencies within the given subcorpus of the respective (POS- or mixed-trigram) top-500 native English trigrams. Finally, to measure distance between each learner language variant and native English, we compute the *cosine similarity* between each of the non-native vectors and native English. Results appear in figure 1.

We see that – as expected – for both models, and for all L1s, low-proficiency learner English variants differ the most from native English. Furthermore, the gap between low and medium proficiency is always bigger than that between medium and high. It is likely that many of the differences between medium and high proficiency are too subtle to be captured by the mixed-model trigrams and manifest rather on the side of appropriate lexical choice within the same POS category.

We see further that similarity for the POS-models is generally higher than for mixed-models, and that especially the gap between low and medium is more pronounced for mixed trigrams.

Among those languages whose low- and medium-level variants are most dissimilar to native English are mainly non-Indo-Germanic languages such as Japanese, Korean and Chinese.

One should note that the proficiency level of an essay is based on a score that also integrates aspects of an essay that cannot be grasped by a trigram model, such as discourse structure; this limits the extent to which we can capture proficiency with our model. Furthermore, while we tried to compare corpora that are as similar as possible in the sense that they both contain argumentative essays, some of the dissimilarities might stem from structural differences like e.g. the topics of the essays in the corpora.

We also compare on a per-essay level with native English, by building one feature vector per essay and comparing to the feature vector for the complete native English corpus.

The results (cf. figure 2) confirm the effects observed per subcorpus. On average, similarity per essay is lower than similarity per subcorpus, which can be explained by the high number of features; not all of the top-500 trigrams occur in every essay. In addition, when aggregating counts over a subcorpus, over- and under-usages of individual trigrams in individual essays tend to cancel each other out. The overall trend confirms that higher-proficiency individual essays are closer to native English than lower-proficiency essays.

5.2 Study 2: Identifying L1-specific deviations in trigram distributions

In Study 1, we show that low-proficiency non-native Englishes are more different from native English on the mixed-model trigram level than medium or high-proficiency variations. We next investigate how different ETS subcorpora (i.e. different combinations of L1 and proficiency level) differ from one another. More specifically, we introduce the *trigram usage factor (TUF)* metric, which computes the relative frequency for an individual trigram across two language variants. TUF allows us to identify individual trigrams which are especially characteristic of par-

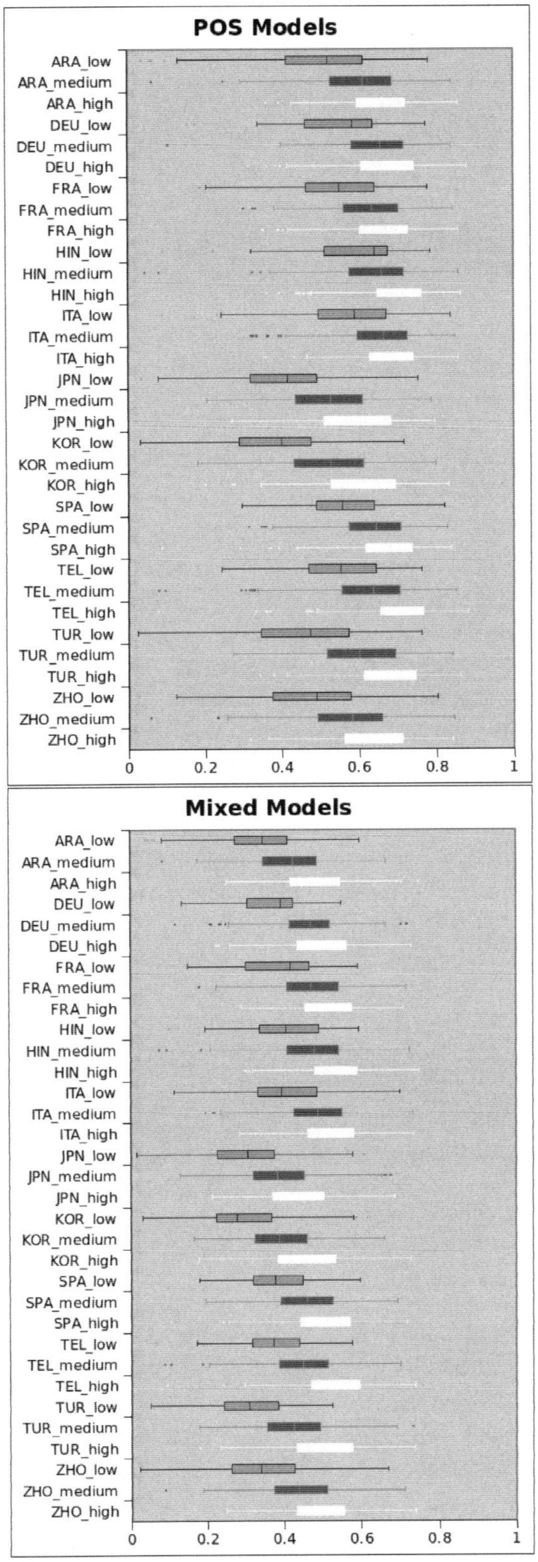

Figure 2: Cosine similarity between non-native English variants and native English, computed *per essay*, using both POS-trigrams (top) and mixed-trigrams (bottom)

ticular L1-proficiency learner groups.

Trigram Usage Factor. To measure how individual trigrams deviate from native English, we compute for each trigram the *usage factor* for a language-proficiency combination by dividing the relative frequency of the trigram t for the relevant subcorpus by the relative frequency of t in native English.

$$\mathrm{TUF}_{Native}(t) = \frac{\mathrm{FREQ}_{L_1\text{-}proficiency}(t)}{\mathrm{FREQ}_{Native}(t)}$$

For example, a usage factor of 4.2 for the trigram *VVP JJ NN* for low-proficiency Japanese means that this trigram occurs 4.2 times more often in essays by low-proficiency Japanese writers than in native English essays.

In the course of this analysis, it became clear that many trigrams are generally overused by most L2 subcorpora, such as *<SENT> for NN*, where *<SENT>* stands for the start of a sentence. We interpret these trigrams as reflecting properties of learner language that are not specific to a particular L1. Table 3 shows the top 10 most overused learner language mixed model trigrams (computed by taking all ETS subcorpora together) as compared to native English. We checked small samples of 10 instances of each of the 10 trigrams for 4 languages (German, French, Japanese, Turkish) and found that they almost never indicated errors, but correspond to frequent sentence constructions such as *I think that*, *for example*, etc as well as influences from the prompt (e.g. many instances of *young people X* and *old people X* in essays asking for a statement about the sentence *Young people enjoy life more than older people do.*).

Over- and underusages for certain phenomena and learner groups are well-known from the Second Language Acquisition literature (e.g. Odlin and Jarvis (2004)). In order to see differences between individual L1s better, we perform an alternative evaluation that is not susceptible to trigrams that are generally frequent learner language. In this variant, we compute TUF relative to the average usage across all L2 essays, by dividing the relative frequency of a trigram t for a given language-proficiency subcorpus by the relative frequency of t in the complete ETS corpus.

$$\mathrm{TUF}_{Learner}(t) = \frac{\mathrm{FREQ}_{L_1\text{-}proficiency}(t)}{\mathrm{FREQ}_{Learner}(t)}$$

overusage factor	trigram	example	rank in LOCNESS
6.01	<SENT> for NN	For example	446
5.15	, i VVP	, I agree	479
4.00	<SENT> i VVP	I believe	169
3.63	i VVP that	I think that	274
2.86	VVP to VV	try to explain	85
2.84	for NN ,	for instance,	179
2.75	JJ NNS VVP	young people enjoy	130
2.65	<SENT> in NN	In conclusion	206
2.62	VVP not VV	do not agree	199
2.51	<SENT> RB ,	Finally,	201

Table 3: The top-10 most overused mixed model trigrams in general learner language as compared to native English

In doing so, we are better able to pick up differences between the different L1s, by measuring whether a certain trigram is over- or underused according to the average usage by language learners.

Study 2a: Trigram Usage Factors in Comparison to Native English

Next, we check how the usage factors of trigrams compared to native English evolve over proficiency levels. We say that a usage factor for a certain trigram evolves *towards native English*, if the usage factor for that trigram moves closer to 1 (i.e. closer to the relative frequency of the trigram in native English) over the three different proficiency levels, e.g. 0.3 for low, 0.4 for medium and 0.8 for high proficiency learners, or 3.5 (low), 2.0 (medium) and 1.3 (high). To account for cases where, for a given trigram, values for the three proficiency levels are not all on the same side of 1, we map values above 1 to their inverse. (This then covers, e.g., cases where an extreme underusage for low-proficiency moves via a moderate underusage for medium, towards only a slight overusage for high proficiency (e.g. 0.3 (low), 0.8 (medium), 1.05 (high, mapped to 0.952)). We still want to consider such cases as moving towards the native distribution, in contrast to a set of usage factors like the following that does not move towards English: 0.3 (low), 0.8 (medium), 1.5 (high, mapped to 0.67)

We perform two versions of this evaluation. In the first (marked as *all* in figure 3), we consider all three proficiency levels. The second evaluation (*low/medium*) is motivated by the cosine similarity results seen in study 1, where the distances between low and medium proficiency are more pronounced than those between medium and high proficiency. In the second evaluation, we ask how often low proficiency moves via medium towards native, excluding the high-proficiency level. We call cases that evolve towards native English where the low-proficiency usage factor is below 1 an underusage, otherwise an overusage.

If we consider all three proficiency levels, we can see that for (on average) 41% of the most frequent 500 native POS trigrams and 42% of the mixed trigrams, TUFs indeed move towards native English. In the second condition, 67% of all POS-trigrams and 65% of all mixed-trigrams move towards native English. (If usage factors varied randomly, we would expect 25% for all three levels and 50% for two levels.) The improvements are similar across languages and across the two trigram models. We see more under- than overusages. We assume that this might be because language learners use a small syntactic inventory quite often, while not exploiting the complete syntactic variety of a language.

Study 2b: Trigram Usage factors Compared to General Learner English: Case studies

We next have a closer look at the most over- and underused trigrams for the medium (i.e. medium-proficiency) level for each of four languages and try to identify properties of the L1 that might account for such overusages. (For underusages, it is generally hard to find examples where a certain trigram should have been used, but wasn't.)

We select German, French, Japanese and Turkish for closer inspection, with these languages

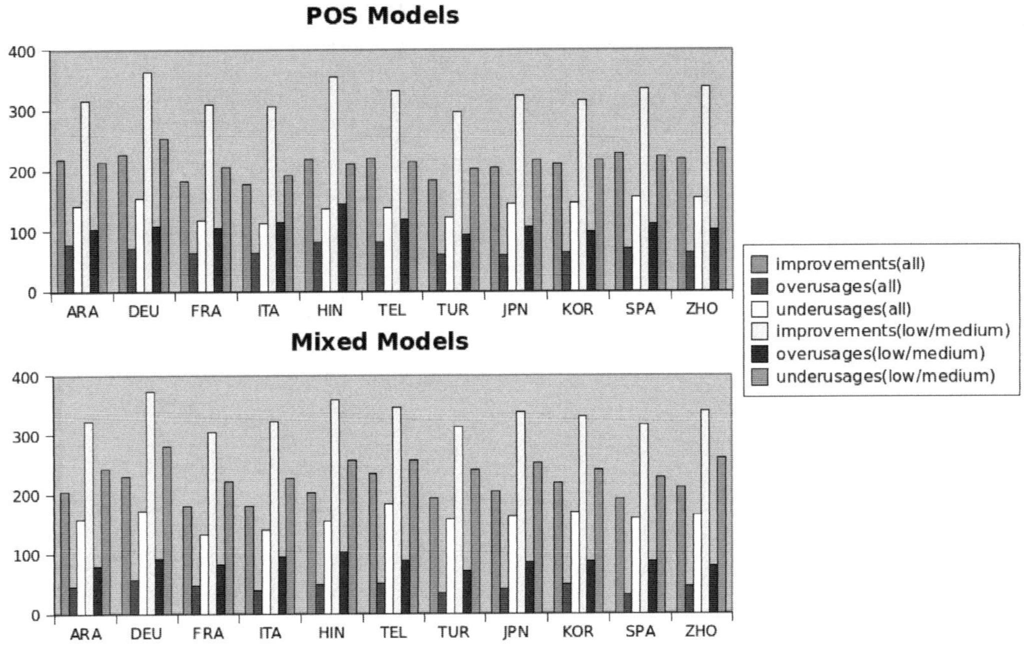

Figure 3: Number of POS and mixed model trigrams (out of the top 500) that moved to a distribution closer to native English

chosen to cover different language families and in order to pick languages of which at least one of the authors has some basic understanding. We choose the medium proficiency subcorpus for each language as it is always the largest subcorpus.

Table 4 shows the top-10 overusages per language, measured against general learner language.

German: In the case of German, the top-2 overused trigrams seem to stem from a tendency not to put a comma after an adverbial phrase at the beginning of a sentence, as in example (1) in contrast to (2).[5]

(1) At this **point it is** good ...

(2) At this point, it is good ...

Additionally, we see overusages of trigrams that correspond to certain fixed phrases such as example (3) or (4).

(3) **<SENT> Another (example|point| reason|...)** ...

(4) **<SENT> On the** other hand ...

[5]Bold print is always used for the relevant trigram in an example sentence from the ETS Corpus. Examples without bold print are constructed.

Interestingly, for low-proficiency German learners we see an underusage of some trigrams involving *will*. This could be explained by the fact that in German, the future is often expressed using a present tense verb, e.g. (5) instead of (6),[6] leading to essay sentences like (7).

(5) *Ich fahre morgen nach Frankfurt.*
$*$ I go to Frankfurt tomorrow.

(6) *Ich werde morgen nach Frankfurt fahren.*
I will go to Frankfurt tomorrow.

(7) Only then **the development is** also in the future as fast as then now.

French: When looking at the top 10 overused trigrams in French, one can observe a high number of trigrams containing infinitive verb constructions like, among others, *VBZ to VV*, *to VB JJ* or *, to VV*. Such a distribution could either point to a high number of infinitive constructions in French as compared to English or to the absence of infinitive constructions and thus an exaggeration of the usage of such structures during learning. However, we could not find evidence for either of the one being the case.

[6]Examples shown with literal translations.

rank	German	French	Japanese	Turkish
1	NN it VBZ	it VBZ a	<SENT> first ,	can not VV
2	NN i VVP	<SENT> that VBZ	, there VBP	<SENT> as a
3	<SENT> another NN	, to VV	i VVP with	<SENT> JJ of
4	VH a JJ	VBZ to VV	<SENT> therefore ,	JJ of all
5	to VH a	when you VVP	i VVP to	<SENT> if you
6	not JJ to	and to VV	VVP not VH	RBS JJ NN
7	to VV this	to VV ,	can VV JJ	VVG the NNS
8	RBR JJ to	to VB JJ	NN , i	this NN ,
9	NP NP NP	NN , we	, i VVP	the NNS ,
10	<SENT> on the	NN , you	NN to VVG	as a NN

Table 4: The top-10 most overused mixed model trigrams in the medium level of four L1 variants of learner language as compared to learner language in general

One can, however, see another trend in the top-ranked trigrams. Contrary to general learner language, French speakers tend to overuse constructions with *you* and *we*. In the top 15 trigrams, two contain *you* (*when you VVP* and *NN , you*) and two *we* (*NN , we* and *we can VV*), e.g. (8) and (9). These could indicate that French speakers adopt a different perspective when writing argumentative texts. One possible reason for this could be the indefinite pronoun *on* in French that – in colloquial, spoken situations – often replaces the morphologically more complex *nous* form of the verb, e.g. (10). In written situations, its purpose is rather to refer to unknown or generalized entities or to replace the use of the passive voice, as in (11) and (12). This ambiguity could be an explanation of the learners' difficulty to choose the appropriate pronoun.

(8) When we are young it is very useful to try a lot of subject but **when you grow** up things change.

(9) In your **argumentation , we** will present some elements in order to give our own opinion.

(10) *On va / Nous allons à la plage.*
We go to the beach.

(11) *On m'a demandé de te donner cela.*
I was asked to give you this.

(12) *On ne sait jamais ...*
One never knows ...

Japanese: For Japanese learners, we see an overusage of trigrams involving formulaic language (*First, ...*) and repetitions of the prompt. The third most overused trigram (*i VVP with*) arises almost exclusively from phrases like (13) and (14). The second most overused sequence covers almost exclusively existential constructions like *there is* or *there are*.

(13) **I agree with** this statement.

(14) **I disagree with** this statement.

A trigram like *can VV JJ* (together with other top 20 Japanese overused trigrams such as *not VV JJ* or *VH JJ NN*) points at problems with article usage, which can be explained by the absence of articles in Japanese. While there are of course valid instantiations of such patterns such as (15), other occurrences of these trigrams actually point at errors such as (16), (17) or (18).

(15) Young people **can do many** things.

(16) They can **get good mark**.

(17) Old people [...] **have long life** expectancy.

(18) Young people do **not feel strong** relationship.

Turkish: In Turkish, there are no definite articles, which results in learner texts with an interesting distribution of trigrams involving *the*. Among the top 30 overused trigrams in Turkish, 7 contain *the* (e.g. *VVG the NNS*, *the RBS JJ*, and *the NNS ,*). One can observe a steady trend for these trigrams across proficiency levels. While low proficiency learners' trigram distribution ranges between under- to slight overusage, medium and high levels strongly overuse them. This is a possible manifestation of a learner's behavior when dealing with a grammatical feature that is nonexistent in their mother tongue – at a low level, they tend to not use it due to a lack of knowledge and confidence. At a higher level, they may overcompensate by trying to fit it in places where it is syntactically or semantically incorrect.

When looking at underused trigrams, what is striking is that half of the top 20 underused trigrams involve the use of a preposition like *for, to, in, with* or *by*. This effect is not surprising as in the Turkish language adpositional phrases are constructed differently than in English or in many Indo-European languages. First of all, Turkish is a strictly head-final language which uses postpositions instead of prepositions. Secondly, English prepositions cannot be – in many cases – directly mapped to their most obvious counterpart in Turkish. The Turkish dative and locative case, for instance, replace certain prepositional phrases in English. The dative case often conveys a sense of movement, e.g. (19), while the locative case is used to refer to a static position as in (20). These examples show how Turkish differently treats temporal and spatial relations that are conveyed by English prepositional phrases.

(19) *Ankara'ya gidiyorum.*
Ankara'[dat.] go[pres.][1.p.sg.]
I'm going to Ankara.

(20) *Ankara'da yaşıyorum.*
Ankara'[lok.] live[pres.][1.p.sg.]
I live in Ankara.

Exploring the Potential for Error Detection

The ability to identify heavily over- or underused sequences in learner language via the TUF metric suggests the potential application of automatically detecting errors in learner language. In fact though, strong over- or underusage of a particular trigram by a learner of a particular L1 might in some instances indicate an error, in other instances it is just an overusage of an otherwise correct phenomenon.

When, for example, low proficiency Japanese learners show a heavy overusage of a trigram of the form *VVP JJ NN* some of these instances might indicate a missing article, as we have seen in some of the examples above. There would be of course the alternative that Japanese low-proficiency learners overuse constructions with mass nouns such as *drink cold milk*. On the other hand, some overused constructions might be attributed to simple formulaic language, such as *i VVP* which is often used in constructions like *I think* etc.

To get a better understanding of how well the usage factor metric can be used for error detection, we perform a small, preliminary annotation study. We annotate 10 random instances each for the top-10 overused trigrams for medium German learners, and for the top 10 generally-overused trigrams (with examples taken also from the medium German learner corpus). We check the underlying learner essays for errors within the range of that phenomenon in order to determine whether they are associated with errors, or rather with non-erroneous but overused phenomena.

In this study we found almost all instances of overusages to be grammatical. Only very few pointed at actual errors, while others point at constructions where there is some preferable alternative. Despite poor results from this small pilot annotation, further investigation of this method for detecting errors may be warranted.

5.3 Study 3: Cross-checking learners against German and Chinese native language distributions using tagset mappings

We have seen that trigram deviations vary across L1s, and we have argued that these variations are due to influences from the L1. In this next study, we investigate a question that naturally arises from this claim that low-proficiency learners are indeed "closer" to their native language (even when writing in a second language) than are high-proficiency learners. The question is whether we observe the opposite trend when comparing L2 essays to texts written natively in the L1.

In order to test this hypothesis, we compute similarities between the non-native (ETS) and native (LOCNESS) English data and two additional native corpora, the German Falko corpus and the Penn Chinese Treebank (see Sec. 3), in order to compare to one language from the same language family (Germanic) and another language that is typologically (and phylogenetically) quite far from English.

The domain of the Falko essay corpus are argumentative essays written by students, making the corpus comparable to the ETS data. For Chinese, we use news texts, as we were unable to locate a native language Asian essay corpus.

Computing similarity between L2-English essays and texts written in other languages of course requires some modifications to the model. First, mixed models are not relevant for obvious reasons; we are limited to the pure POS models. Second, because different languages generally use different POS tagsets, we need to map these tags into a common representation. For this we use the universal POS tagset proposed by Petrov et al. (2012) and existing scripts for mapping various tagsets (including Penn Treebank, STTS for German and Penn Chinese Treebank) into the following 12 coarse-grained POS tags: "NOUN (nouns), VERB (verbs), ADJ (adjectives), ADV (adverbs), PRON (pronouns), DET (determiners and articles), ADP (prepositions and postpositions), NUM (numerals), CONJ (conjunctions), PRT (particles), . (punctuation marks) and X (a catch-all for other categories such as abbreviations or foreign words)".

We then evaluate by building feature vectors for native English, German and Chinese by taking all mapped POS trigrams for that corpus into consideration and computing pairwise similarity between these three corpora and the per-language subcorpora from ETS (see figure 4).

The comparison with native English via POS-mapped trigrams confirms that the increasing similarities for higher-proficiency L2 writing still show on the coarser level of mapped trigrams. We see a similar pattern to that in figure 1.

The comparison with the German data shows a slightly different picture. For the non-European languages Arabic, Hindi, Japanese and Korean, we see a similar behavior as for English: with increasing proficiency students' writing also comes closer to native German. We argue that this might be due to the close relatedness between German and English as two Germanic languages. For Telugu, Turkish and Chinese this pattern is only valid for low and medium proficiency while European languages (except for a tendency in French) do not show this behavior. Unexpectedly, high-proficiency German learners are closer to native German than low-proficiency Germans, maybe an effect of coming closer to the full expressiveness of Germanic languages.

In the comparison with Chinese, we can see that similarity is generally lower than for German or even native English, and we observe that other

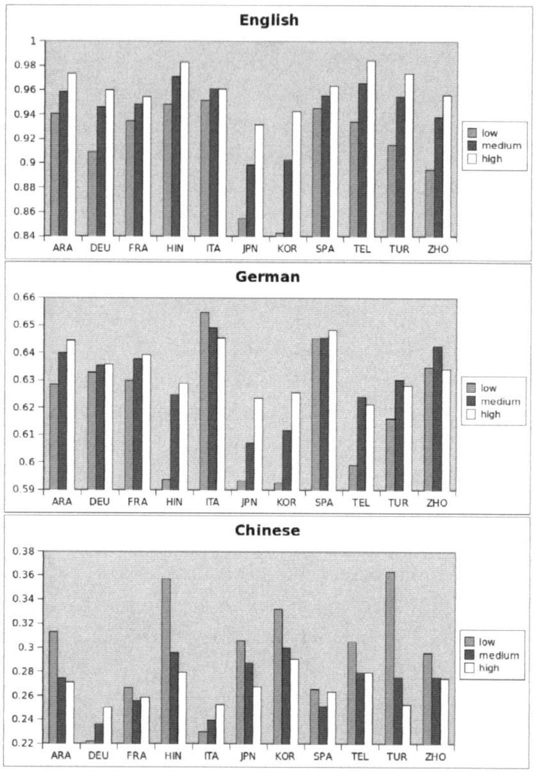

Figure 4: Cosine similarity between non-native English variants and native English (top), German (middle) and Chinese (bottom) on the level of mapped POS trigrams

Asian languages generally have a higher similarity with Chinese than do European languages. In order to exclude this lesser similarity stemming from domain effects instead of language effects, we also compared to the German TIGER corpus (Brants et al., 2004) of newspaper texts and found similarities in a range comparable to Falko (interestingly, the similarities were higher for TIGER than for Falko), with very similar tendencies for the individual L1 subcorpora.

These observations of similarities between language families echos findings by Nagata and Whittaker (2013), who reconstruct Indo-European language family relations from language models of non-native writings.

5.4 Study 4: Exploring the Use of Trigram Models for Proficiency Classification

We have shown that different L1s as well as different proficiency levels lead to different trigram frequency distributions that deviate from those for native English. As a final exploratory experi-

Features	general	L1 specific
baseline	68.8	70.5
top 500 trigrams	46.7	48.9
baseline + top 500 trigrams	46.5	49.7
selected attributes (all)	69.8	**71.5**
selected attributes (trigrams)	59.1	62.9

Table 5: Averaged classification accuracy when training on datasets for individual L1s and on mixed corpora

ment, we begin the investigation into whether vectors from our mixed models are beneficial for the task of automatic proficiency classification into the three proficiency levels low, medium and high.

While both lexical and POS trigrams have been used in related work on automatic grading of learner texts (Yannakoudakis et al., 2011), we are specifically interested in investigating the effectiveness of L1-specific classifiers.

We operationalize this question using two different feature sets. We use a baseline that consists of just 5 features: number of tokens, number of sentences, average number of tokens per sentence, number of individual types and type-token-ratio. Additionally, we use the frequencies of the most frequent 500 native English trigrams as features.

For classification, we train an out-of-the-box logistic regression model using the WEKA toolkit (Hall et al., 2009). We train and evaluate classifiers per L1, using all 1100 (per language) essays and leave-one-out cross-validation. For comparison, we additionally sample 11 disjoint "general" sets of 1100 essays from all 11 languages, with equal amounts of essays per language in each subcorpus. We use the same cross-validation procedure in order to have training corpora of compatible size. We use each of the two features sets individually and combined (cf. table 5)

This baseline is already very strong, and the new trigram features (both alone and in combination) perform far worse than the baseline. However, all feature combinations benefit from L1 specific classifiers.

A plausible reason for this degradation in performance is the excessive number of features. Thus we employ feature selection to identify the best performing features. Specifically, we use WEKA's CfsSubsetEval attribute selection method to identify the most helpful features from both the trigrams and the baseline features. If we use these features for classification (thus simulating an optimal classifier for a dataset), we get improvement from the trigram features over the baseline and again see a better performance for the L1 specific models over the general models.

We take these first results as an indicator that proficiency classification can further profit from L1 information and will investigate this classification task further in future work.

6 Conclusions and Future Work

In this paper we have shown how two important factors influencing EFL writings, L1 and proficiency level, influence the shallow syntactic structure of essays. Using frequency vectors of trigrams, we investigate various attributes of learner language, using both cosine similarity and our own trigram usage factor metric. We hope this framework will be useful for further investigations into learner language, automatic error detection, and automatic proficiency classification.

What we have not covered so far in our experiments is a third important factor: the influence of the task, in our case the essay prompt. In the course of performing the case studies and annotation pilot described here, we have seen that the prompt can be visible even on the abstraction level of POS models. For example, students that write essays in response to the prompt (21) frequently reused the prepositional phrase *In twenty years*, which resulted in higher frequency counts for the POS trigram *PP CD NNS*.

(21) Do you agree or disagree with the following statement? *In twenty years, there will be fewer cars in use than there are today.* Use reasons and examples to support your answer.

In future work we therefore plan to use clustering techniques to measure the influence that each of the three influence factors (L1, prompt and proficiency level) have on the trigram distributions of essays and to explicitly quantify the influence of the prompt.

7 Acknowledgements

We would like to thank three anonymous reviewers for their helpful comments. We also thank Annemarie Friedrich for fruitful discussions and Helmut Schmid and Richard Eckart de Castilho for their valuable comments regarding our work with Treetagger. This work was funded by the Cluster of Excellence 'Multimodal Computing and Interaction' of the German Excellence Initiative. The third author is supported by SFB-732 'Incremental Specification in Context'.

References

Daniel Blanchard, Joel Tetreault, Derrick Higgins, Aoife Cahill, and Martin Chodorow. 2014. ETS corpus of non-native written English.

Sabine Brants, Stefanie Dipper, Peter Eisenberg, Silvia Hansen, Esther König, Wolfgang Lezius, Christian Rohrer, George Smith, and Hans Uszkoreit. 2004. TIGER: Linguistic interpretation of a German corpus. *Journal of Language and Computation, Special Issue*, 2(4):597–620.

Martin Chodorow and Claudia Leacock. 2000. An unsupervised method for detecting grammatical errors. In *Proceedings of the 1st North American Chapter of the Association for Computational Linguistics Conference*, NAACL 2000, pages 140–147, Stroudsburg, PA, USA. Association for Computational Linguistics.

Mark Hall, Eibe Frank, Geoffrey Holmes, Bernhard Pfahringer, Peter Reutemann, and Ian H. Witten. 2009. The WEKA Data Mining Software: An update. *SIGKDD Explor. Newsl.*, 11(1):10–18, November.

Matthieu Hermet and Alain Désilets. 2009. Using first and second language models to correct preposition errors in second language authoring. In *Proceedings of the Fourth Workshop on Innovative Use of NLP for Building Educational Applications*, pages 64–72. Association for Computational Linguistics.

Mitchell P Marcus, Mary Ann Marcinkiewicz, and Beatrice Santorini. 1993. Building a large annotated corpus of English: The Penn Treebank. *Computational linguistics*, 19(2):313–330.

Ryo Nagata and Edward W. D. Whittaker. 2013. Reconstructing an Indo-European family tree from non-native English texts. In *Proceedings of the 51st Annual Meeting of the Association for Computational Linguistics, ACL 2013, 4-9 August 2013, Sofia, Bulgaria, Volume 1: Long Papers*, pages 1137–1147. The Association for Computer Linguistics.

Terence Odlin and Scott Jarvis. 2004. Same source, different outcomes: A study of Swedish influence on the acquisition of English in Finland. *International Journal of Multilingualism*, 1(2):123–140.

Slav Petrov, Dipanjan Das, and Ryan McDonald. 2012. A universal part-of-speech tagset. In *Proc. of LREC.*

Marc Reznicek, Anke Lüdeling, and Franziska Schwantuschke. 2012. Das Falko-Handbuch: Korpusaufbau und Annotationen: Version 2.0.

Anne Schiller, Simone Teufel, Christine Stöckert, and Christine Thielen. 1999. Guidelines für das Tagging deutscher Textcorpora mit STTS. Technical report, IMS-CL, University Stuttgart.

Helmut Schmid. 1994. Probabilistic part-of-speech tagging using decision trees. In *Proceedings of International Conference on New Methods in Language Processing*, Manchester, UK.

Larry Selinker. 1972. Interlanguage. *International Review of Applied Linguistics in Language Teaching*, 10(1–4):209–232.

Guihua Sun, Xiaohua Liu, Gao Cong, Ming Zhou, Zhongyang Xiong, John Lee, and Chin-Yew Lin. 2007. Detecting erroneous sentences using automatically mined sequential patterns. In *Proceedings of the 45th Annual Meeting of the Association of Computational Linguistics*, pages 81–88, Prague, Czech Republic, June. Association for Computational Linguistics.

Joel R Tetreault and Martin Chodorow. 2009. Examining the use of region web counts for esl error detection. In *Web as Corpus Workshop (WAC5)*, page 71.

Joel Tetreault, Daniel Blanchard, and Aoife Cahill. 2013. A report on the first native language identification shared task. In *In Proceedings of the Eighth Workshop on Innovative Use of NLP for Building Educational Applications.*

Sze-Meng Jojo Wong, Mark Dras, and Mark Johnson. 2012. Exploring adaptor grammars for native language identification. In *Proceedings of the 2012 Joint Conference on Empirical Methods in Natural Language Processing and Computational Natural Language Learning*, pages 699–709. Association for Computational Linguistics.

Nianwen Xue, Fu-Dong Chiou, and Martha Palmer. 2002. Building a large-scale annotated Chinese corpus. In *Proceedings of the 19th International Conference on Computational Linguistics - Volume 1*, COLING '02, pages 1–8, Stroudsburg, PA, USA. Association for Computational Linguistics.

Helen Yannakoudakis, Ted Briscoe, and Ben Medlock. 2011. A new dataset and method for automatically grading ESOL texts. In *Proceedings of the 49th Annual Meeting of the Association for Computational Linguistics: Human Language Technologies - Volume 1*, HLT '11, pages 180–189, Stroudsburg, PA, USA. Association for Computational Linguistics.

Semi-automated typical error annotation for learner English essays: integrating frameworks

Andrey Kutuzov
National Research University
Higher School of Economics
akutuzov@hse.ru

Elizaveta Kuzmenko
National Research University
Higher School of Economics
eakuzmenko_2@edu.hse.ru

Abstract

This paper proposes integration of three open source utilities: *brat* web annotation tool, *Freeling* suite of linguistic analyzers and *Aspell* spellchecker. We demonstrate how their combination can be used to pre-annotate texts in a learner corpus of English essays with potential errors and ease human annotators' work.

Spellchecker alerts and morphological analyzer tagging probabilities are used to detect students' possible errors of most typical sorts. F-measure for the developed pre-annotation framework with regard to human annotation is 0.57, which already makes the system a substantial help to human annotators, but at the same time leaves room for further improvement.

1 Introduction

Nowadays, learner corpora accumulating typical learner texts together with typical errors often support language learning. They allow researching into inter-relation of L1 and L2, and the process of language acquisition in general. Error annotation of such corpora is particularly valuable as it can provide various insights into the features of learners' interlanguage and contribute to error analysis. For example, errors made by a learner convey a lot of information about how (s)he acquires a foreign language, and which categories are most problematic (Corder, 1981). Another promising feature of error annotation is the possibility to detect L1-specific errors (Nesselhauf, 2004). Also, error-tagged corpora help human annotators and teachers who are grading students' works. All this consequently leads to more efficient language learning process.

Annotating learner texts with common linguistic annotation layers (tokens, morphology, syntax, etc) is challenging because of the non-conventional nature of such texts. It is not easy to find out what was the author's intended utterance (target hypothesis) and how it should be marked up in the corpus. Sometimes several 'readings' are possible, further complicating the situation. As for the error annotation in learner corpora, being a very complicated and a time-consuming process, it is often put aside.

Meanwhile, these two problems can be merged into one solution. Non-canonical features of learner texts can be of use when finding and correcting errors and revealing text structure. 'Strange', unconventional spelling or morphological forms provide clues about mismatches between the target hypothesis and surface form of the text (Ragheb and Dickinson, 2012). Therefore, it is possible to perform some types of error annotation automatically, disregarding its complexity.

In this paper we demonstrate our approach towards semi-automated pre-annotation of typical errors in learner English texts. We propose a solution to facilitate learner corpora error annotation based on integrating three well-known open-source frameworks, particularly, *Aspell*, *Freeling* and *brat*.

The paper is structured as follows. In Section 2 we give an overview of other approaches to automatic error annotation, and how our approach differs from them. In Section 3 we describe the tools employed in the framework, testing corpus and general workflow. Section 4 gives details on the system performance in comparison to human-annotated texts. Section 5 points at a working prototype available online and briefly describes implementing the same tool-chain in one's own environment. Finally, in Section 6 we conclude and describe directions of further research.

Andrey Kutuzov and Elizaveta Kuzmenko 2015. Semi-automated typical error annotation for learner English essays: Integrating frameworks. *Proceedings of the 4th workshop on NLP for Computer Assisted Language Learning at NODALIDA 2015*. NEALT Proceedings Series 26 / Linköping Electronic Conference Proceedings 114: 35–41.

2 Related work

The idea of automatic error annotation is not new. Overview of approaches to automated error detection in learner corpora can be found, for example, in (Leacock et al., 2010). In the recent years, there have been a few attempts to solve this problem, and all of them proposed unique solutions, so there are no established methods. Particularly, one should mention the methods deployed in the CzSL corpus (Hana et al., 2010) and in the Falko corpus (Reznicek et al., 2013).

In the CzSL corpus (the corpus of Czech as a Second Language) the workflow of annotating errors is bound by the peculiarities of the annotation scheme. The annotation scheme consists of the two tiers, or layers. The first tier includes errors dealing with the form of a word instance, so spelling and orthographic errors are defined to this tier as well as morphological errors (words with incorrect inflectional affixes). The second tier contains errors that can be derived from the context. Therefore, lexical and syntactic errors fall into this category.

As for the process of automatic error annotation, it is applied mostly to the errors from the first tier (Jelínek et al., 2012): words are compared to the dictionaries of canonical Czech, and if discrepancies are found, such word forms are marked as errors. It is specific for the devised automatic annotation tools that possible morphological errors are not only manifested by tags, but the tags are further subspecified by the word part in which the possible error is found. An original word form and a word form from the dictionary are compared symbol by symbol, and if alternations are found in the inflectional part of the word, this counts as a morphological error; if the word form contains mistake in its stem part, it is considered to be a made-up word (Rosen et al., 2014).

This automatic annotation system is used not only to extend the manual annotation, but also to verify it. If the system finds some words that are unknown to the morphological analyzer but are unmarked with tags, the errors were possibly overlooked by a human annotator. If the changes proposed by the system concern pronunciation, the presence of the tag denoting inflection or word base is checked.

All texts in CzSL are also pre-processed with *Korektor* spell-checker (Hana et al., 2014). It is applied to both original and corrected versions of the text.

This automatic spell-checking is similar in part to what we do in this research. However, we additionally introduce automatic error-tagging using morphosyntactic tags (see Section 3)

Errors from the second tier are annotated manually in CzSL; however, some information is added to them automatically, based on the context of the error, or, in case of an error in a compound verb form, on the morphological analyses assigned to the word. It happens only when a human annotator has already initially marked the errors.

Our approach is different in two ways. First, our framework detects not only errors from the first tier, but also the errors from the second tier (e.g., agreement errors), which are annotated manually in CzSL. The mismatch in the context of word form in the case of disagreement reflected in morphological analysis allows us to detect more error types than by using only spellchecker. Second, we do not distinguish between different types of spelling errors. As English is not a highly inflective language like Czech, spelling errors convey less information about their nature; most often it means that the word detected by a spellchecker simply does not exist.

The Falko corpus (Reznicek et al., 2013) performs error-annotation using the mismatch between target hypothesis (speaker's intention) and the actual learner's text. For example, in the sentence '*The girl sing loudly.*' the target hypothesis formulated by a sequence of queries into a corpus of native speakers' texts states that such noun phrase should be accompanied by a verb with the -*s* ending, and there are no cases when such combination of word forms is met in the native language. Nevertheless, if this form is found in the learner's text, this span is marked as an error.

This approach is partly similar to a component of our framework, the one which is based on morphological analysis. As we will demonstrate in Section 3, we derive the target hypothesis from the PoS tags probabilities, and not from a corpus of canonical English, but the nature of the approach stays the same.

3 Mixing tools and the corpus

To construct our framework, we used three tools: an annotation framework, a set of linguistic analyzers and a spellchecker.

Brat (Stenetorp et al., 2012) is an open-source

framework for web-based text annotation. It separates documents from their markup (see below), and allows several people to annotate a text simultaneously, using only their web browsers. It also provides an important possibility to easily define new annotation schemes. In this paper, it serves as a basis for all other tools.

Freeling (Padro and Stanilovsky, 2012) is a set of open source linguistic analyzers for several languages. It features tokenizing, sentence splitting, morphology analyzers with disambiguation, syntax parsing, named entity recognition, etc. In this research, we use only morphological analyzer for English.

Finally, *GNU Aspell*[1], currently maintained by Kevin Atkinson, is one of the most popular open source spelling correction utilities. It compares an input word to a set of dictionaries and if the word is out-of-vocabulary (possible typo), provides a list of words similar in spelling.

The tools are tested on REALEC, Russian Error Annotated Learner Corpus[2]. REALEC is a corpus of Russian students' essays written in English (Kuzmenko and Kutuzov, 2014). The works in the corpus are written by 2, 3 and 4 year students from National Research University Higher School of Economics, Faculty of Philology, together with students of the first year of Masters program, Faculty of Psychology. The texts are mostly routine assignments or exam-type essays. Most of the works are written with the premise to prepare for the IELTS examination and have the structure similar to that of IELTS writing tasks (Moore and Morton, 2005). Essays in this corpus are manually error-annotated in *brat* by human experts (mostly English teachers). They output a substantial amount of quality annotation, but the process of error spotting is rather cumbersome and time-consuming. Thus, there is a certain need to at least semi-automatize this annotation task and make computers do the most monotonous part of the work.

The work flow we propose is as follows. When a document (an essay) is uploaded to the system, it is processed by *Freeling*. Processing includes tokenizing, sentence splitting and morphological analysis (lemmatizing and PoS-tagging).

Then, we detect possible errors. First, all tokens and lemmas generated by *Freeling* are checked with *Aspell*. If neither token nor lemma are known English words, we assign this token an attribute '*Possible spelling error or typo*', which is visible and searchable in the annotators' web interface. We also add a note to this token with the first correction suggested by *Aspell*. Thus, L2 (English in this case) spelling rules are the basis for this annotation.

It is important that by design *Aspell* does not make any difference between non-words or unknown neologisms and typos (misspelled words). This sometimes may lead to false flags: for example, the word '*polysemy*' is out of vocabulary and marked as a spelling error, with '*polysemous*' suggested as a correction. We plan to deal with this issue in the future, most probably using evaluation of Damerau-Levenshtein distance (Damerau, 1964) between words and suggestions.

After annotating spelling errors, we move on to the Part-of-Speech (PoS) tags for all tokens.

In the course of morphological analysis, *Freeling* outputs probabilities of different PoS tags for each token, depending on its lexical environment. For example, in the sentence

'*He plays with his phone.*'

Freeling assigns the token '*plays*' the PoS tag **VBZ** (Verb, 3rd person singular present) with probability as high as 0.663934. However, if we introduce an error in the same sentence and transform it into

'*He **play** with his phone.*',

the token '*play*' is assigned the **VBP** tag (Verb, non-3rd person singular present) with the probability as low as 0.163539.

The reason of such a low value is that other tagging variants for this word form are much more probable. We can get all the possible morphological 'readings' of the given word with their default probabilities in the model. Continuing our example with '*play*', *Freeling* had to choose from three variants (given with their respective probabilities):

1. **VB 0.565684** (Verb, base form)
2. **NN 0.270777** (Noun, singular)
3. **VBP 0.163539** (Verb, non-3rd person singular present)

Most probable tag for '*play*' is an infinite verb form. However, a variant with low default probability was chosen because of the context (preceding '*He*'), thus signaling that something erroneous

[1] `http://aspell.net/`

[2] `http://realec.org`

may be happening here. Naturally, in the case of the correct sentence, the PoS tag **VBZ** for the word '*plays*' has the maximum default probability:

1. **VBZ 0.663934** (Verb, 3rd person singular present)
2. **NNS 0.336066** (Noun, plural)

This information gives some clues as to which words manifest possible errors. Particularly, we check whether there are other possible tagging variants with default probability greater than the probability of the variant *Freeling* actually chosen. If it is true, we suppose that *Freeling* met difficulties in choosing between tag variants, and there can be a mismatch between word surface form and its distributional features (lexical environment). In this case we assign an attribute '*Possible grammar or morphology error*' to this token. As such tokens can be highly ambiguous with regard to their tagging variants, a note with other tags (rejected by *Freeling*) is added to the token annotation.

Of course, this issue is not tackled with 100% precision, and low default probability of the chosen tag variant does not always mean that there is an error in the sentence. However, as we show below, in most cases this is a good indicator of inconsistencies in the word sequence, and this can help an annotator a lot. Some proportion of mistakes is necessarily acceptable, and the output will afterwards be checked by a human, so that incorrectly flagged instances will be removed from the annotation.

After having conducted the pre-annotation of errors, the output of *Freeling* and *Aspell* is converted to the standard CONLL format and then to the *brat* standoff annotation format. At this stage text and annotations are separated (consistent with the data structure adopted in Falko). The only change in the text is introduced by tokenization, which extracts all punctuation marks and surrounds them with spaces, so that they can be considered full-fledged tokens. All annotations are kept in a separate annotation file for each document, linked to the actual text by character offsets.

Surprisingly, the shallow analysis described above returns quite satisfactory results with regards to recall and the number of false flags; see Section 4 for evaluation of our technique.

As a result, human expert receives a document which is not only tokenized and POS-tagged, but also pre-annotated with possible errors. The errors caught by this method are mostly limited to misspellings, typos and morphosyntactic ones. Nevertheless, these types constitute a substantial share of errors in a real learner corpus.

Consequently, our system allows annotators to spend less time on spotting spans to pay attention to, and additionally lessens the risk of overlooking errors. The latter turned out to be particularly useful, as human annotators tend to miss the spelling errors in which some letter doubles or, on the contrary, double lettering is absent. For example, errors like '*signalling*' (gerund form), or '*posess*' were overlooked in human annotation, but found by the framework.

Also, paradoxically, automatic error annotation helps to detect errors which are not spotted by humans because of the transfer effect from their L1. For instance, Russian learners of English often make an error concerning the verb *consider* control pattern. Many learners generate erroneous *consider smth as smth*, which comes from the analogous structure in Russian, but is ungrammatical for English. Human annotators tend to omit this error, but it is always found by the framework.

4 Evaluation

Our pre-annotation was tested against errors spotted by human annotators in 800 documents from REALEC corpus (213 694 word tokens in total). After applying the framework, we encountered 10490 morphological errors 'issued' by *Freeling* and 3018 spelling errors by *Aspell*. This is consistent with the ratio of spelling mistakes in human annotations of the same texts (Kuzmenko and Kutuzov, 2014).

Initially, we checked strict coincidences of automatically detected 'pre-errors' with human-annotated error spans, so that only the tokens from our pre-annotation that exactly match those assigned by humans were counted. Quite expected, performance was not very impressive, with F-measure only 0.05 (see Table 1).

The reason for such low values is that human experts often mark spans ranging across several words or even parts of words. In fact, tagging several words is necessary for particular types of errors, for example, word order errors. At the same time, our system annotates only separate words, and thus lags behind humans.

The figures for *Aspell* and *Freeling* parts of the framework separately were discouraging as well.

While the *Freeling* component in general performs slightly better that the *Aspell* component, both tools demonstrate low recall and even more discouraging precision.

However, in fact we do not need precise hits into human annotated spans. What we expect is that pre-annotation will help an expert or a language teacher in spotting problematic areas in the text, and then they will be properly annotated.

Hence, we measured how good our system is at hitting right sentences, that is, generating errors at the same sentences where human experts found various mistakes.

First, we carried out evaluation of our system with regard to a simple baseline, within which we assigned an error mark to every sentence in the corpus with the probability of 50%. This alone resulted in increased performance, with F-measure 0.123 (see Table 1).

When we applied the real *Freeling* and *Aspell* output, we received results seriously outperforming the baseline, with precision and recall at values allowing real-world usage (0.46 and 0.75 respectively).

Table 1: Performance in comparison with human judgments

	Precision	Recall	F-measure
	Strict matches		
Overall	0.04	0.07	0.05
Aspell only	0.007	0.04	0.01
Freeling only	0.046	0.06	0.05
	Sentence-wise matches		
Baseline	0.0973	0.169	0.123
Overall	0.4637	**0.7479**	0.57
Freeling only	**0.7643**	0.5383	**0.63**

This is already a decent result as precision is relatively high, therefore, most of the errors spotted by the system are flagged correctly, and an annotator only needs to define a proper error type for them.

It can be seen that the integration of *Aspell* slightly spoils the precision figures. *Freeling* method without spell-checking provides better precision and F-measure. This is due to the fact that *Aspell* assigns erroneous tags to the instances, being driven by the wide definition of an error as a word form absent in its dictionary. At the same time, *Aspell* helps achieving very high recall values.

It should be mentioned that *Korektor* spellchecking system for Czech is reported in (Hana et al., 2014) to perform with an accuracy of 74%. It is difficult to compare performance of spellcheckers for English and Czech. However, increasing the performance of our spellchecker part should definitely be an important step towards enhancing our framework in general.

Nevertheless, recall has increased, and almost 75% of sentences containing errors are already flagged even before experts take to their job; this reduces human efforts. The overall precision is lower, meaning that about a half of flags are false: we pre-annotate an error within a sentence, where according to human experts there are no errors.

For example, in the sentence

'*Since that period modern human started to tame animals and use them for the good of primitive society.*'

our framework finds three errors: in the words *that*, *tame*, and *use*. Meanwhile, only one error was identified by manual annotation: erroneous choice of a lexeme *started* in this context. For now, we do not set up a goal to identify lexical errors, but the annotation of redundant tokens clearly is a disadvantage for an annotator.

There are also positive examples. In the sentence

'*Hen was spread worldwide by humans, and that's why domestication was useful for these species.*'

the number of errors found by our system and by human annotators equals to four in both cases, and in two cases (the words *these* and *spread*) pre-annotation and manual annotation coincide (Actually *was spread* and *these species* are annotated by humans, but the problematic area is identified correctly).

We plan to improve precision in future research. For now, this issue is mitigated by the fact that in the case of incorrect pre-annotation, an expert can easily change or ignore it. We consider precision at the value of 0.5 to be acceptable for the time being.

5 Implementation

Our implementation of the described system can be found at `http://dev.rus-ltc.org/learner_preprocess/index.xhtml#/integration/`. It is possible to browse through a sample of REALEC texts with possible errors marked by red. After logging in with the user name '*learner*' and identical password, one can upload own texts. They will be tagged and annotated with possible mistakes.

Deploying this framework on one's own server is as easy as installing *brat* and *Freeling* and slightly fixing *brat* document workflow to include pre-processing stage. *GNU Aspell* is usually already installed on any Unix/Linux system. All the source code for our converters and detectors together with instructions is available online at Github[3].

6 Conclusions

We presented a framework integrating morphological analyzer, spellchecker and web annotation tool in order to pre-annotate learner English texts with possible errors. While already providing a significant relief to human experts, with F-measure 0.57 in relation to human annotations, it is yet to be extended and improved.

It is important that unlike other automatic error-tagging systems (for example, in (Hana et al., 2010)), our framework functions without any knowledge about target hypotheses or correct forms of words in the analyzed texts. Its input is raw learner-generated sentences and it does its work before any human intervention. Additionally, the errors we detect are not limited to incorrect word forms, but also include error classes related to complex syntactic patterns.

One of prospective directions for improving our system performance is to differentiate between a larger number of error types, for example, taking into account syntax trees constructed by *Freeling* parser module and finding non-typical dependencies. Supposedly, this can help in spotting errors on supra-lexical levels.

Tracking lexical errors can be done comparing neighbors of a given unit in canonical English language corpora and our learner corpus. Also, spellchecking part can be augmented with additional dictionaries, especially containing gazetteers of named entities, in order to prevent it from incorrectly marking proper names as typos.

Also, we plan to investigate the relationship between the language level of learners' and the features of their mistakes from the perspective of automatic annotation process. It is expected that the architecture of the automatic annotation system is heavily dependent on the linguistic characteristics of texts. For example, in the beginners' level it is possible that more mistakes concerning morphology and syntax are found, whereas advanced learners make more lexical mistakes. Therefore, we plan to adapt different algorithms and approaches towards automatic error annotation to different levels on language knowledge.

Another improvement that is needed to be done in future is to test human reaction on the errors spotted automatically. For now, our system was not deeply tested and checked with English language teachers, and we need to measure to what extent such pre-annotation facilitates human efforts and how many errors spoil the process of correct error annotation.

[3] `https://github.com/akutuzov/error_annotation`

References

Stephen Pit Corder. 1981. *Error analysis and interlanguage*, volume 112. Oxford Univ Press.

Fred J. Damerau. 1964. A technique for computer detection and correction of spelling errors. *Commun. ACM*, 7(3):171–176, March.

Jirka Hana, Alexandr Rosen, Svatava Škodová, and Barbora Štindlová. 2010. Error-tagged learner corpus of czech. In *Proceedings of the Fourth Linguistic Annotation Workshop*, pages 11–19. Association for Computational Linguistics.

Jirka Hana, Alexandr Rosen, Barbora Štindlová, and Jan Štěpánek. 2014. Building a learner corpus. *Language Resources and Evaluation*, 48(4):741–752.

Tomáš Jelínek, Barbora Štindlová, Alexandr Rosen, and Jirka Hana. 2012. Combining manual and automatic annotation of a learner corpus. In *Text, Speech and Dialogue*, pages 127–134. Springer.

Elizaveta Kuzmenko and Andrey Kutuzov. 2014. Russian error-annotated learner english corpus: a tool for computer-assisted language learning. *NEALT Proceedings Series Vol. 22*, page 87.

Claudia Leacock, Martin Chodorow, Michael Gamon, and Joel Tetreault. 2010. Automated grammatical error detection for language learners. *Synthesis lectures on human language technologies*, 3(1):1–134.

Tim Moore and Janne Morton. 2005. Dimensions of difference: a comparison of university writing and ielts writing. *Journal of English for Academic Purposes*, 4(1):43–66.

Nadja Nesselhauf. 2004. Learner corpora and their potential for language teaching. *How to use corpora in language teaching*, 12:125–156.

Llus Padro and Evgeny Stanilovsky. 2012. Freeling 3.0: Towards wider multilinguality. In Nicoletta Calzolari, Khalid Choukri, Thierry Declerck, Mehmet Uur Doan, Bente Maegaard, Joseph Mariani, Jan Odijk, and Stelios Piperidis, editors, *Proceedings of the Eight International Conference on Language Resources and Evaluation (LREC'12)*, Istanbul, Turkey, may. European Language Resources Association (ELRA).

Marwa Ragheb and Markus Dickinson. 2012. Defining syntax for learner language annotation. In *Proceedings of COLING 2012: Posters*, pages 965–974, Mumbai, India, December.

Marc Reznicek, Anke Lüdeling, and Hagen Hirschmann. 2013. Competing target hypotheses in the falko corpus. *Automatic Treatment and Analysis of Learner Corpus Data*, 59.

Alexandr Rosen, Jirka Hana, Barbora Štindlová, and Anna Feldman. 2014. Evaluating and automating the annotation of a learner corpus. *Language Resources and Evaluation*, 48(1):65–92.

Pontus Stenetorp, Sampo Pyysalo, Goran Topic, Tomoko Ohta, Sophia Ananiadou, and Jun'ichi Tsujii. 2012. brat: a web-based tool for nlp-assisted text annotation. In *EACL*, pages 102–107.

Short Answer Grading: When Sorting Helps and When it Doesn't

Ulrike Pado and Cornelia Kiefer
HFT Stuttgart
Schellingstr. 24
70176 Stuttgart
ulrike.pado@hft-stuttgart.de

Abstract

Automatic short-answer grading promises improved student feedback at reduced teacher effort both during and after instruction. Automated grading is, however, controversial in high-stakes testing and complex systems can be difficult to set up by non-experts, especially for frequently changing questions. We propose a versatile, domain-independent system that assists *manual* grading by pre-sorting answers according to their similarity to a reference answer. We show near state-of-the-art performance on the task of automatically grading the answers from CREG (Meurers et al., 2011). To evaluate the grader assistance task, we present CSSAG (Computer Science Short Answers in German), a new corpus of German computer science questions answered by natives and highly-proficient non-natives. On this corpus, we demonstrate the positive influence of answer sorting on the slowest-graded, most complex-to-assess questions.

1 Introduction

Recent research on short-answer prompts has focussed mostly on fully automatically predicting student scores (Burrows, Gurevych and Stein (2015)). While research interest has intensified, central problems in practice remain: On a technical note, teachers need to quickly set up reliable automatic grading for frequently changing questions, which is not always feasible for complex systems. An even more basic concern is that the use of an automated system in summative testing (which determines pass or fail or the overall grade for a class) may not be compatible with legal constraints and with student and teacher beliefs about fair grading.

Another issue with short-answer questions themselves is the objectivity of grading – will two different teachers or even the same teacher on two different days award the same number of points to the same answer? Mohler, Bunescu and Mihalcea (2011) present results from the preparation of their test corpus where their judges perfectly agreed on a score 58% of the time, with differences of one point (out of five) in another 23% of cases. This opens a teacher up to justified complaints from students on 19% of questions. Objective, replicable grading therefore is a big concern in teaching, and of course even more so in summative testing. It is also one that can be naturally addressed with the help of automated or semi-automated systems.

We believe that short-answer grading in real-world teaching will not profit most from fully automatic grade prediction. Instead, relatively simple NLP techniques that need little or no domain adaptation to deal with new questions can assist *manual* grading and both improve objectivity and minimize effort.

We present such a grading assistance tool that presents student answers for manual correction ranked by their similarity to the reference answer (or answers). The intuition is that graders will profit from seeing clearly correct and clearly incorrect answers together.

The similarity scores are computed on the lemma level, so that the system is portable to any other language where a lemmatiser exists. Since it only relies on the lexical content of student and reference answer, it is completely independent of a question domain. To further facilitate real-world use, it is packaged as a plugin to the open-source Learning Management System (LMS) Moodle[1] to allow easy use for teachers.

For the purpose of evaluating our system, we in-

[1] www.moodle.org

Ulrike Pado and Cornelia Kiefer 2015. Short answer grading: When sorting helps and when it doesn't. *Proceedings of the 4th workshop on NLP for Computer Assisted Language Learning at NODALIDA 2015.* NEALT Proceedings Series 26 / Linköping Electronic Conference Proceedings 114: 42–50.

troduce Computer Science Short Answers in German (CSSAG), a new data set of nine short-answer questions from the Computer Science domain. Answers were collected from native or near-native speakers and double-annotated (grading conflicts were resolved after annotation by discussion between the annotators). We report our observations about structural differences between the answers to a native-speaker content matter task (as in CSSAG) and a reading comprehension task that primarily tests language skills (as exemplified by the German standard corpus CREG-1032, Meurers, Ziai, Ott and Kopp (2011)).

We evaluate our system in two ways. First, we adapt our ranking task to binary classification and perform classic score prediction (as correct or wrong) for the CREG-1032 and CSSAG data sets. Our shallow tool approximates the state of the art in binary classification for CREG, with a small drop in performance on CSSAG. This shows that the similarity scores carry relevant information for predicting human grades.

Our second evaluation directly addresses our intended task of grader assistance. Time and accuracy data from human graders shows that the ranking of student answers is beneficial especially for questions that are very slow to grade, at no reduction in agreement with gold grades. Further exploration shows that the slow-to-grade questions are worth more points, which indicates that the teacher expects more complex answers. Higher answer complexity entails more difficult grading. Presenting the answers to these questions ranked by similarity to the reference answer results in a simulated speedup of more than 10%.

2 Related Work

The comprehensive overview over the short-answer grading by Burrows et al. (2015) traces the deepening interest in this task over recent years. Burrows et al. identify different eras in short-answer grading represented by clusters of papers that share a common theme. The first short-answer assessment systems worked with the mapping of concepts in student and reference answer. A prominent example is C-Rater (Leacock and Chodorow, 2003), which attempts a rule-based matching of concepts in the student and reference answers. Answers are first normalised on different levels, using, e.g., spell-checking, synonyms and anaphora resolution.

Analogously to trends in general Computational Linguistics, a later important strategy is the use of corpus-based methods that aim to estimate student answer-reference answer similarity from large collections of language data. The first paper from this group describes the Atenea system (Alfonseca and Pérez, 2004; Pérez et al., 2005), which makes use of distributional (vector-space) and surface-based (BLEU) similarity measures derived from large corpora to assess short-answer questions.

Another theme is the use of pattern matching and alignment on different representational levels. As a system for German, an especially relevant example is CoSeC-DE (Hahn and Meurers, 2012). Hahn and Meurers derive underspecified formal semantic representations of question, student and reference answer and use information structure to identify given and new information in the answers. They derive a score based on quality estimates for the alignment of the representations. Their system reaches the highest prediction accuracy for the German standard corpus CREG.

Corpus-based and alignment-based similarity measures are often used as features in the era of machine learning. The machine-learning based paper most relevant for us is CoMiC-DE, the system for German by Meurers et al. (2011). The system uses alignments on various levels of linguistic representation like tokens, chunks, or dependency parses, as well as corpus-based similarity measures to train a memory-based learner. This paper also introduces the CREG corpus, which we further analyse below.

Burrows et al. explicitly define their subject as *automatic* short answer grading, and the vast majority of publications on short answer grading aim for fully automatic grade prediction. We did, however, consciously choose to build an assistance system for *manual* short answer grading.

Two such grader assistance systems have been presented, to our knowledge. Both independently propose the clustering of answers; grading then proceeds per cluster instead of per answer to reduce manual effort. Basu, Jacobs and Vanderwende (2013) use machine learning to train a model of similarity between student answers using vector-based similarity and lexical match features. These similarity scores are then used to hierarchically cluster the answers, allowing teachers to grade multiple answers at the same time and provide detailed feedback on classes of (possibly erroneous) answers. Basu et al. show that their system reaches 92.9% accuracy in automated binary classification on their 10-question English content-assessment data set. They also find a drastic reduction in the number of actions a grader has to take in order to grade all student answers: 40-50% of simulated actions can be saved to reach the same grading result as answer-by-answer grading.

In a follow-up paper, Brooks, Basu, Jacobs and Vanderwende (2014) present a user study for the system. Overall, teachers were able to assign a grade to every answer three times as quickly with the system, while their agreement with the gold score did not suffer.

Horbach, Palmer and Wolska (2014) cluster student short answers flatly using surface features (word and character n-grams, presence of predefined core keywords). They make the explicit assumption that a small number of incorrectly graded items is acceptable as long as the teacher's workload is greatly reduced. They evaluate on German learner listening comprehension material: Using their system, a simulated teacher can reach 85% agreement with the gold score by labelling only 40% of responses.

3 The Grader Assistance System

Our system relies on determining the similarity of student and reference answer and then sorting the student answers according to this similarity. In contrast to Horbach et al. (2014) and Basu et al. (2013), we do not cluster student answers, because teachers need to see every single answer in order to make the tool acceptable for use in summative assessment.

The similarity score is computed on filtered lemmas from the student and reference answer. Further, we demote words from the question (Mohler et al. (2011)) to only retain content word lemmas that are relevant to the new content in the student or reference answer. This is a shallow approximation of content rather than surface form. Note, however, that so far, we do not include synonyms nor handle paraphrases. At this point, our goal was to evaluate a very simple, versatile system which does not need domain adaptation.

Table 1 shows the processing steps for an example question. The analysis system uses the DKPro Core (de Castilho and Gurevych, 2014) and DKPro Similarity (Bär, Zesch and Gurevych (2013)) libraries. We compute lemmas using the Stanford lemmatiser component in DKPro Core (Manning, Surdeanu, Bauer, Finkel, Bethard and McClosky (2014)) and exclude stop words using Porter's German stop word list[2]. We then exclude all lemmas from the student and reference answer that already appear in the question. The similarity between student and reference answer is calculated using the DKPro Similarity implementation of Greedy String Tiling (as proposed by Wise (1996)). This text similarity measure aims to find (the longest possible) matching substrings, regardless of position in the original text, and ranges between 0 (no match) and 1 (perfect agreement).

If more than one reference answer is provided, the similarity of the student answer to all variants of reference answers will be calculated and the highest score will be used.

The system is implemented as a plugin to the LMS Moodle[3] and available under the GPL. The implementation can easily be ported to other LMS, as well.

4 CSSAG (Computer Science Short Answers in German)

We collected a data set of nine short-answer questions and answers collected over the course of a one-semester Introduction to Programming in Java class aimed at first-year undergraduate students. The questions test students' knowledge of basic object-oriented programming concepts. In week 5, for example, students had to explain the relationship between classes and objects (German question: "Erklären Sie den Zusammenhang zwischen Klassen und Objekten."). Students are native speakers of German or have sufficient German skills to pursue higher education exclusively in German.

There are a total of 491 answers, with an average of 55 answers per questions (min 33, max 83) and at least one reference answer meant for human graders. Answers are one to three sentences long.

Each question was graded (out of one or two points in increments of 0.5 points) by two experienced graders who are domain experts. Cases of disagreement were adjudicated by discussion between the graders; when necessary, the reference answer was disambiguated or extended. No an-

[2]http://snowball.tartarus.org/algorithms/german/stop.txt

[3]https://github.com/HftAssistedGrading/moodle-plugin-assisted-grading

Frage: Erklären Sie den Zusammenhang zwischen Klassen und Objekten
Question: Explain the relationship between classes and objects.

	Reference Answer	Student Answer
Original	Eine Klasse ist der Bauplan für ein Objekt. Ein Objekt ist eine konkrete Instanz einer Klasse. *A class is the blueprint for an object. An object is a concrete instance of a class.*	Eine Klasse ist ein Bauplan für ein Objekt. Die Klasse definiert den Typ des Objektes. Ein Objekt ist eine Ausprägung *A class is a blueprint for the object. The class defines the type of the object. An object is a realisation.*
Lemmas, no stopwords	klasse bauplan objekt objekt konkret instanz klasse	klasse bauplan objekt klasse definieren typ objekt objekt ausprägung
Question demotion	bauplan konkret instanz	bauplan definieren typ ausprägung

Table 1: Processing steps in the Grader Assistance system.

swers were excluded from the corpus.

We intend to make the data set publicly available for research.

5 Experiment 1: Binary Classification

Our evaluation is two-fold: Our first experiment establishes that the similarity between student and reference answers does indeed predict human-assigned grades. We then go on to test the influence of ranking the student answers on grading speed and agreement with the gold grade.

In Experiment 1, we classify student short answers as correct or incorrect given their similarity to the reference answer. This is the classical automatic short answer grading task given a two-level scoring regime. We compare our results against Hahn and Meurers (2012) who report the best results to date on CREG, the German short-answer corpus. Their system runs a deep semantic analysis to derive underspecified formal semantic representations of the question, student and reference answer and determine information structural focus.

5.1 Data

In addition to CSSAG, we use the CREG-1032 corpus as described in Meurers et al. (2011). It contains German learner answers to reading comprehension questions.

5.2 Method

We use the similarity scores to classify answers as correct or wrong by determining a similarity threshold. Scores above the threshold are taken to indicate a correct answer (due to its large similarity to the reference answer), scores below the threshold are counted as incorrect answers.

System	CREG	CSSAG
Frequency Baseline	50.0	64.6 (strict) 53.4 (generous)
Grader Assistance	83.7	78.0 (strict) 80.0 (generous)
Meurers et al. ('11)	84.7	–
Hahn&Meurers ('12)	86.3	–

Table 2: Exp. 1: Results for binary classification by the Grader Assistance system on the CREG-1032 and CSSAG data sets.

The threshold was set a priori at 0.49 as the mid-point of the similarity scale. The value was checked for plausibility on a held-out question from the CSSAG data set (question ID w4). The threshold was, however, not optimised for either corpus, so further improvements may be possible when the threshold is adapted. Empirically setting the threshold poses the interesting problem of sampling a representative development set, since the set should not overlap with the test data and there is considerable variation between the different questions.

The CREG data set can be evaluated right away given the threshold, as answers are either fully correct or incorrect. On the CSSAG data set, partial credit was awarded. We therefore report two scoring methods: *strict* scoring counts only answers with full points as correct, *generous* scoring counts answers with full or partial points as correct.

5.3 Results and Discussion

Table 2 reports the results. We compare the systems against the frequency baseline for each data set (i.e., the prediction accuracy for always predicting the most frequent class). The CREG data are constructed to contain exactly half correct and half incorrect answers, so the frequency baseline on this data set is 50%. On the CSSAG data, the bias of the scoring methods is clearly visible: The strict method only counts those answers as correct that were assigned full points. About two thirds of the student answers are consequently classed as incorrect, and the frequency baseline (when predicting "incorrect") is much higher than for the generous scoring method, where answers with partial points also count as correct. For generous scoring, the frequency baseline is close to 50%.

Our grading assistance system reaches roughly 84% accuracy on the CREG-1032 data set. This comes close to the best result to date, 86.3% reported for the deep Hahn and Meurers (2012) CoSeC-DE system. Our shallow analysis is thus able to roughly approximate the state-of-the-art. Apparently, the corpus contains only a small portion of answers that are graded incorrectly by the shallow method and need to be deeply analysed for accurate scoring. We discuss this observation further in Section 5.4.

On the CSSAG data set, the system accuracy reaches 78% for strict and 80% for generous interpretation of partial points. While these numbers are noticeably lower than on the CREG data set, the system clearly outperforms the frequency baselines. It gains noticeably more over the generous baseline than over the strict baseline: It appears to be easier for our simple string similarity strategy to distinguish between wrong and (partially) correct answers than to tell apart partially correct and fully correct answers. In any case, the results imply a meaningful relation between similarity to the reference answer and human-assigned grade.

5.4 Corpus Comparison

Further analysis of the test corpora revealed interesting differences in their characteristics. We find that the correct answers in CREG are generally very similar to the reference answer, markedly more so than for the CSSAG data.

To estimate the variance within the answers, we report the average similarity score between student and reference answers as computed by our system in Table 3. For CREG, answers have an average similarity score of 0.39 to the reference answer. This number even goes up to 0.65 for just the correct answers. With the CSSAG corpus, the average score over all answers is much lower at 0.27 (or 0.54 for the answers with full gold scores).

Corpus	All Questions	Correct Questions
CREG	0.39	0.65
CSSAG	0.27	0.54

Table 3: Corpus comparison: Average similarity of student answers to reference answer in CREG and CSSAG corpora. CSSAG correct answers by strict interpretation of points assigned.

The high similarity of correct student answers to the reference answer explains the success of our shallow method in classifying CREG answers: Simple string matching to the reference easily reveals the correct answers.

In general, the higher CREG similarity scores indicate much less variance among the answers in CREG than in CSSAG. This empirical finding is at odds with the usual theoretical assumptions about short-answer questions: Limited answer variance is a hallmark of closed question types like fill-in-the-blank, while short answer questions are seen as an open question type with generally high answer variation. Our results imply that within a theoretically open question type, there is a range of actual answer variation. To our knowledge, this observation is new in the literature, although it clearly has repercussions for automatic grading or grading assistance, with more open questions being more difficult to treat. Evaluation results should therefore be interpreted in the context of answer variation in the test data: The results that can be expected from deep and shallow models respectively depend on the amount of variation in the answers relative to the reference answer, with little variation favouring shallow models.

One contributing factor to the closedness of CREG questions is that the corpus contains only answers that were graded consistently by all annotators. This means that the classification as correct or incorrect is very certain, but the distinction is artificially made more clear-cut than it really is. CSSAG in contrast contains all available student answers, with grader inconsistencies addressed by grader discussion after the initial annotation.

Apart from design decisions, there are also linguistic and psycholinguistic reasons for more answer variation in CSSAG: There is a difference both in tasks and student population. In the reading comprehension task reflected in the CREG data, students have all recently read the same text and are presumably primed by its lexical and syntactic features (Meyer and Schvaneveldt, 1971; Bock, 1986). This means they are more likely to use the same words and structures in their answers (Pickering and Garrod, 2004), even if explicit answer lifting (copying from the text) is not considered. In addition, learners may lack the vocabulary and language skills to paraphrase freely. In contrast, the CSSAG questions assess mastery of content taught several days previously, and the students are mostly native speakers, with the non-natives skilled enough to pursue higher education exclusively in German. This student pool produces a wider range of paraphrases of the correct answer.

In sum, the high similarity of the correct CREG answers allows a rough content matching algorithm such as ours to reach the performance of linguistically more complex systems. An interesting question for further research is to evaluate the performance of the more complex systems on the CSSAG data set. With more varied answer phrasing, the complex strategies may show more pronounced gains.

6 Experiment 2: Agreement and Speed in Grading

Our second evaluation tests the influence of similarity ranking on grading accuracy and speed. This is the task for which we designed the system.

6.1 Method

We presented a group of twelve graders with all questions, reference answers and student answers from CSSAG. Four graders were highly experienced, the other eight were novice graders, but all were knowledgeable in the domain.

The answers were either ordered randomly or sorted according to their similarity to the reference answer. Each grader saw roughly half the questions in sorted and half in random order. This means that each question was annotated by six graders in each of the two conditions. Graders were not informed that some of the answer sets had been sorted, and sorted and random answer sets were in chance order in the work packages. Graders were timed for each question. We had to discard the times for one grader because they were registered incorrectly. We then computed grader agreement with the gold grade and average grading time per answer.

6.2 Results and Discussion

Average agreement of the points assigned by the graders to the gold grades (gold agreement) was comparable between the two groups of graders, although, not surprisingly, the expert graders did somewhat better at 75.7% agreement, compared to 73.4% for the novice graders[4]. The novices took roughly 1.4 times longer for grading than the experts (14.7 vs. 10.5 seconds per answer).

Comparing the random and sorted conditions averaged across all graders yields an interesting picture: Sorting has only a small positive effect on grader agreement with the gold grade at 73.8% agreement in the random condition and 74.6% in the sorted condition. Average grading time is identical (13.6 seconds random, 13.6 seconds sorted).

The grading agreements for the same question across conditions are highly correlated (Spearman's $\rho = 0.92, p < 0.01$) with similar means, implying that there is no influence of our sorting scheme on grader agreement.

In the random condition, there is a significant negative correlation between grading time and agreement ($\rho = -0.795, p < 0.02$), so that answers that are graded more accurately are also quicker to grade. However, this correlation does not hold in the sorted condition. Also, the grading time for the two conditions is not significantly correlated ($\rho = 0.588, p = 0.08$) despite the equal averages. This shows that the sorting does have an effect on grading time, even though the effect appears to be zero-sum, since it does not show in the condition average.

In the sorted condition, we find a significant correlation between grading time and the average similarity score for a question ($\rho = 0.798, p < 0.02$) instead of the correlation between time and agreement in the random condition. Given sorting, a question will be graded faster if the average answer similarity to the reference is low. This is the case for example if there are a great number of fragment answers that are easy to score (as incor-

[4]"Novice" only refers to grading experience; all graders were knowledgeable in the question domain

Question ID	Random	Sorted	Δ
w7	8	12	4
w10	10	13	3
w4	11	9	-2
w6	12	12	0
pvl2	12.4	14	1.6
pvl3	13.2	11	-2.2
w5	13.5	21.4	7
Average	13.6	13.6	0
w9	**20**	**14**	**-6**
w11	**22**	**16**	**-5**

Table 4: Exp. 2: Average grading times in seconds per condition. Slowest questions gain most from sorting.

Question ID	Δ s	Points
pvl2	1	1.6
w4	1	-2
w5	1	7
w6	1	0
w7	1	4
w10	1	3
pvl3	**2**	**-2.2**
w9	**2**	**-6**
w11	**2**	**-5**

Table 5: Exp. 2: Maximum points per question and time difference between random and sorted conditions. Two-point questions (in bold) show speedup (negative difference).

rect). Scoring all of these answers together seems to free up time for grading the answers with relevant content.

Table 4 shows which questions profit mostly from sorted presentation: We list the average grading times for each question in the random and sorted conditions and the time difference between conditions. The average grading time over all questions is given, as well. The lines in the table are sorted by grading duration in the random condition. The table suggests that the answers that are slower than average to grade gain most by a sorted presentation (by about five seconds per answer). Answers that are faster than average to grade or take average time do not profit from sorting.

This implies that optimally, we should present questions that will be slow to grade in sorted order, and questions that will take average time or less in random order. This raises the question of how to identify the slow-to-grade questions beforehand. Further scrutiny of the questions reveals that speedup by sorting is achieved mainly for those questions where students can earn two points (rather than one, as for the majority of questions). Table 5 shows the questions with their maximum number of points to be earned and the time difference achieved by sorting (a negative difference is a speedup).

Choosing the presentation mode according to the points students can gain for each question has the advantage of relying only on information that is available for every question out of the logic of the task, so no further manual or automatic processing of the questions is required.

Two-point questions differ from one-point questions in the cognitive load on the grader: When creating the question, the teacher already expected complex answers with several facets that are each worth partial points. The grader needs to keep track of all expected and actually given aspects of the answer in order to arrive at the final score. In this cognitively demanding situation, sorting yields speed gains of 15-30% per question.

If the questions had been presented optimally to our graders (answers to one-point questions in random order, answers to two-point questions in sorted order), the average overall grading time per answer would be 12 seconds (based on the experimental by-question averages from the sorted and random conditions). This is a 12% gain, equivalent to 13 minutes saved when grading the total of 491 answers. Agreement with gold grades would be virtually unaffected at an average 73.5% across all questions (as opposed to an average 73.8% in the random condition). Further, only presenting the answers to some questions in sorted order should also help to avoid graders' possible over-reliance on the similarity score for grading once they become aware of the sorted presentation. Future work will test the efficacy of the hybrid presentation mode in practice.

7 Conclusions and Future Work

In this paper, we have presented a system to assist manual grading of short-answer questions by ranking student answers in order of their similarity to the reference answer. The system is designed to be domain-independent and easy to use for teachers without computational linguistics expertise. Beside portability and usability, our main goal was to speed up grading and improve objectivity. Our approach ensures that the teacher still sees every student answer, which is an important prerequisite for use of the system in summative testing.

To evaluate our system, we have introduced a new data set, Computer Science Short Answers in German (CSSAG). The data demonstrably differs from the standard German short-answer corpus CREG (Meurers et al., 2011) in several respects: The questions assess content mastery rather than language skills and were collected from native German speakers. We find that the difference in task and student population make CSSAG answers more variable than CREG answers. Further work will investigate equivalent English corpora.

In our evaluation of the automatic grading task, our shallow tool approximates the state of the art in binary classification for CREG, with a small drop in performance on CSSAG. This shows that the similarity scores carry relevant information for predicting human grades. We also hypothesise that the lower answer variation in CREG makes it easier to automatically grade with a shallow system such as ours. Future work should aim to determine whether more complex systems show more performance gains on CSSAG.

Time data from human graders indicates that the ranking of student answers is beneficial especially for questions that are very slow to grade. These are questions with a maximum grade of more than one point, which reflects their greater complexity and, in consequence, the greater cognitive load on the grader. Optimal answer presentation guided by the maximum number of points that can be earned for each question speeds up grading by 1.6 seconds per answer on average, at undiminished agreement with gold. This simulated result needs to be evaluated experimentally in the future.

References

Enrique Alfonseca and Diana Pérez. 2004. Automatic assessment of open ended questions with a BLEU-inspired algorithm and shallow NLP. In *Advances in Natural Language Processing*, volume 3230 of *Lecture Notes in Computer Science*. Springer.

Daniel Bär, Torsten Zesch, and Iryna Gurevych. 2013. DKPro Similarity: An open source framework for text similarity. In *Proceedings of the 51st Annual Meeting of the Association for Computational Linguistics: System Demonstrations*, pages 121–126.

Sumit Basu, Chuck Jacobs, and Lucy Vanderwende. 2013. Powergrading: A clustering approach to amplify human effort for short answer grading. *Transactions of the Association for Computational Linguistics*, 1:391–402.

Kathryn Bock. 1986. Syntactic persistence in language production. *Cognitive Psychology*, 18:355–387.

Michael Brooks, Sumit Basu, Charles Jacobs, and Lucy Vanderwende. 2014. Divide and correct: Using clusters to grade short answers at scale. In *Learning @ Scale*.

Steven Burrows, Iryna Gurevych, and Benno Stein. 2015. The eras and trends of automatic short answer grading. *International Journal of Artificial Intelligence in Education*, 25:60–117.

Richard Eckart de Castilho and Iryna Gurevych. 2014. A broad-coverage collection of portable NLP components for building shareable analysis pipelines. In *Proceedings of the Workshop on Open Infrastructures and Analysis Frameworks for HLT (OIAF4HLT) at COLING 2014*, pages 1–11.

Michael Hahn and Detmar Meurers. 2012. Evaluating the meaning of answers to reading comprehension questions: A semantics-based approach. In *Proceedings of the 7th Workshop on Innovative Use of NLP for Building Educational Applications (BEA7)*.

Andrea Horbach, Alexis Palmer, and Magdalena Wolska. 2014. Finding a tradeoff between accuracy and rater's workload in grading clustered short answers. In *Proceedings of the 9th LREC*, pages 588–595.

Claudia Leacock and M. Chodorow. 2003. C-rater: Automated scoring of short-answer questions. *Computers and the Humanities*, 37(4):389–405.

Christopher D. Manning, Mihai Surdeanu, John Bauer, Jenny Finkel, Steven J. Bethard, and David McClosky. 2014. The Stanford CoreNLP natural language processing toolkit. In *Proceedings of 52nd Annual Meeting of the Association for Computational Linguistics: System Demonstrations*, pages 55–60.

Detmar Meurers, Ramon Ziai, Niels Ott, and Janina Kopp. 2011. Evaluating answers to reading comprehension questions in context: Results for German and the role of information structure. In *Proceedings of the TextInfer 2011 Workshop on Textual Entailment*, pages 1–9.

David E. Meyer and Roger W. Schvaneveldt. 1971. Facilitation in recognizing pairs of words: Evidence of a dependence between retrieval operations. *Journal of Experimental Psychology*, 90(2):227–234.

Michael Mohler, Razvan Bunescu, and Rada Mihalcea. 2011. Learning to grade short answer questions using semantic similarity measures and dependency graph alignments. In *Proceedings of the 49th Annual Meeting of the Association for Computational Linguistics*, pages 752–762. ACL.

Diana Pérez, Enrique Alfonseca, Pilar Rodríguez, Alfio Gliozzo, Carlo Strappavara, and Bernardo Magnini. 2005. About the effects of combining latent semantic analysis with natural language processing techniques for free-text assessment. *Revista Signos: Estudios de Linguïstica*, 38(59):325–343.

Martin Pickering and Simon Garrod. 2004. The interactive-alignment model: Developments and refinements. *Behavioral and Brain Sciences*, 27:212–225.

Michael J. Wise. 1996. YAP3: Improved detection of similarities in computer program and other texts. In *SIGCSEB: SIGCSE Bulletin (ACM Special Interest Group on Computer Science Education)*, pages 130–134. ACM Press.

Oahpa! Õpi! Opiq!
Developing free online programs for learning Estonian and Võro

Heli Uibo
University of Tartu
UiT The Arctic University of Norway
heli.uibo@ut.ee

Jaak Pruulmann-Vengerfeldt
University of Tartu
Cybernetica AS
jjpp@cyber.ee

Jack Rueter
University of Helsinki
rueter.jack@gmail.com

Sulev Iva
University of Tartu
sulev.iva@ut.ee

Abstract

This paper describes porting Oahpa, a set of advanced interactive language learning programs, to two new languages both of which spoken in Estonia – Estonian and Võro. Our programs offer a platform where the user can practice vocabulary and the generation of morphologically complex forms both in isolation and within sentential contexts. An overview of the Oahpa system and its two important building blocks – the morphological finite state transducer and the pedagogical lexicon – is given. The development of morphological finite state transducers for Estonian and Võro, as well as tailoring the specific transducers for pedagogical purposes are described. The adaptation of both Estonian and Võro Oahpa to the target user groups is also discussed.

1 Introduction

1.1 The languages

Estonian is the second largest Baltic Finnic language with approximately 1.2 million native speakers. It has several morphological features common in agglutinative languages. Estonian, however, has had a lot of influence from Swedish, German and Russian, as such it has lost vowel harmony and is shifting towards becoming a fusional language.

Estonian is the only official language in Estonia, and, in many professions, high-level Estonian language skills are required. Free online programs for learning Estonian grammar would contribute to better Estonian language proficiency among the people with other mother tongues in Estonia (31.3% of the whole population in 2011). The motivation to learn the Estonian language is generally high among students and working-age people. Estonian morphology and the use of correct cases are the most difficult things for people with non-Uralic languages as their mother tongues. Therefore, a morphology-aware ICALL system would be a helpful tool for Estonian language learners of all ages.

Recently, a couple of free online language learning environments for Estonian have appeared that are not commercial but require the creation of a user account: keeleklikk.ee and eestikeel.ee. These programs, however, have slightly different foci and target groups compared to Oahpa. They are not very well suited to the needs of university students.

The Võro language belongs to the same branch of the Uralic language family as Estonian and Finnish. Traditionally it has been considered a subset of the South Estonian dialect group of the Estonian language, but nowadays it has its own literary language and the activists of Võro are applying for the recognition of Võro as a regional official language in Estonian. The population of Võro speakers is estimated at 74,400, most of them reside in southeastern Estonia.

At the end of the 1980s a revival of South Estonian varieties started. A new standard of the Võro language was developed by native speakers and activists, linguists and non-linguists alike. The standardisation led to the publication of a bilingual Võro-Estonian dictionary in 2002, containing 15,000 entries, and the Estonian-Võro dictionary in 2014, with 20,000 entries.

A course in the Võro language and local (cultural) history, was taught in 19 schools in the language area in 2012/2013. The Võro language is

Heli Uibo, Jaak Pruulmann-Vengerfeldt, Jack Rueter and Sulev Iva 2015. Oahpa! Õpi! Opiq! Developing free online programs for learning Estonian and Võro. *Proceedings of the 4th workshop on NLP for Computer Assisted Language Learning at NODALIDA 2015.* NEALT Proceedings Series 26 / Linköping Electronic Conference Proceedings 114: 51–64.

taught mostly in primary school, in most cases as an extracurricular activity, but as an elective in nine schools (Koreinik, 2013).

Most teaching materials for the Võro language have been created, published and provided by the Võro Institute. The materials include a reader/textbook (Võrokiilne lugõmik, 1996), a primer (ABC kiräoppus, 1998), a song collection (Tsirr-virr lõokõnõ, 1999), a workbook for the primer, a workbook for the audiotape, a book of local cultural history (Võromaa kodolugu, 2004), an illustrated vocabulary (Piltsynastu, 2004), and a variety of audio and (audio-)visual materials. In addition, there are many texts which can and are being used for teaching: fiction, poetry, a travelogue, print media and an annual series of the children's own creation (Mino Võromaa, since 1987). (Koreinik, 2013)

Since 1996 the Võro language as a subject can be studied at the University of Tartu. Since 2003 the subject has been called "South Estonian I" for beginners, and "South Estonian II" for advanced students. Since 2004 there have been two series of lectures: "Modern Southern Estonian Literature" and "History of the South Estonian literary language". The language of instruction of all these courses is Võro. Some theses and dissertations have also been defended in the Võro language. In 2006 and 2012 it was also taught at the University of Helsinki.

A free online language learning system is very important for the survival of the Võro language. It will be integrated into the curriculum at University of Tartu. At the same time we aim to design the system in a way that would make it usable for individual internet-based learning. This is the only way to learn the Võru literary language for many people because most of the Võro speakers have never learned the language at school; there are still few possibilities for traditional learning and also the literary language is relatively new.

1.2 Oahpa

The ICALL system Oahpa (Antonsen et al, 2009) has been developed at Giellatekno, the centre for Saami language technology at UiT The Arctic University of Norway. The intended target group of Oahpa are adult language learners and it is primarily meant as a supporting tool for learning vocabulary and grammar for a students attending respective language courses.

The pedagogical motivation behind Oahpa was to develop a language tutoring system which

- has free-form dialogues and sophisticated error analysis
- gives immediate error feedback and advice to the user
- is flexible
- is easily integrated into instruction at schools and universities
- enables the choice of main dialect and meta-language
- is freely accessible via the Internet

Oahpa consists of six games: a vocabulary quiz (Leksa) which is based solely on a semantically enriched electronic dictionary, a numeral quiz (Numra) based on a small finite state transducer that generates and recognises numbers, date and time expressions, the morphology drill games Morfa-S (isolated word forms) and Morfa-C (word forms in sentential contexts) that require a morphological finite state transducer, a question-answer drill (Vasta) and a dialogue game (Sahka). The last two games require morphological disambiguation and syntactic analysis on top of the morphological analysis.

The first and so far the only instance of Oahpa that incorporates all the six modules – North Saami Oahpa – can be tried out on the URL http://oahpa.no/davvi/. For some other languages a version of Oahpa with four modules exist – Leksa, Numra, Morfa-S and Morfa-C. We are planning to create Võro Oahpa in the same scale. For Estonian our purpose is to go a step further and also implement the fifth module, Vasta, that assumes morphological disambiguation.

Thanks to a cooperation project between the Universities of Tartu and Tromsø, we can make use of the powerful language technology development infrastructure (Moshagen et al, 2014) that has been set up at Giellatekno, and among other things reuse their technologies of creating ICALL applications.

This paper presents work in progress. The described systems are in the stage of development and most of the modules of both Estonian and Võro Oahpa are still incomplete.

2 The prerequisites for creating Oahpa

In order to set up the above mentioned modules of Oahpa the minimal set of language resources consists of

- a morphology engine, e.g. a morphological finite state transducer (FST),
- a pedagogical lexicon that is enriched with semantic categories and other information that is used in Oahpa.

2.1 Morphology engine

We have chosen finite state transducers as a model for formalising Estonian and Võro, partly because this technology is supported by the Giellatekno infrastructure but also considering its theoretical and performance-related pros and cons.

Most modern natural language processing (NLP) applications perform their tasks using statistical language models. At the same time, for morphologically rich languages, estimation of the language models is problematic due to the high number of compound words and inflected word forms. Thus, rule-based models are better suitable for describing the morphology of highly inflected languages. Another argument for choosing the rule-based methods is the relatively limited amount of electronically available texts for languages such as Estonian with its 1.2 million speakers, and even more, Võro, as its literary language is new.

The attractiveness of the finite-state technology for natural language processing stems from four sources: modularity of the design; the compact representation that is achieved through minimization; efficiency, which is a result of linear recognition time with finite-state devices; and reversibility, resulting from the declarative nature of such devices. (Wintner, 2008)

Moreover, given the pedagogical applications in sight, we were not only interested in automatic morphological segmentation but in a system that would be able to generate the complete and correct morphological paradigm for each lemma in the lexicon. That is, for our application correctness was more important than coverage. The resources of an educational application must be manually revised, otherwise such an application would not make any sense.

2.2 Morphological FST of Estonian

North Saami and Estonian stand out among the Uralic languages as the ones deviating most from the agglutinative type. The net outcome of this is a system of non-concatenative morphology (consonant gradation, diphthong simplification) combined with a small set of reusable affixes. This requires concatenative and suprasegmental transducers being composed as serial transducers in order to represent the morphology in an adequate way (for an analysis of Saami and Estonian see (Trosterud and Uibo, 2005)).

2.2.1 Existing implementations

There are at least three implementations of computer morphology of Estonian but they all share one common basis that was described in the lexicon and grammar parts of Concise Morphological Dictionary (CMD) (Viks, 1992). On one hand, CMD was created in cooperation with computational linguists and is quite formal and easy to implement. On the other hand, CMD deals mostly with morphology of simple words and with some derivational processes but ignores completely compounding which gives approximately 10..20% of the words in Estonian texts. Also, its base dictionary is an outdated normative dictionary which has a lot of old words and words that are used only in some dialects. There are words that no one knows what they mean or where they come from. That means that there are some problems with using this system for modern Estonian both in rules and vocabulary.

The best implementation of Estonian morphology is Estmorf (Kaalep and Vaino, 2000) by Filosoft, with roots in CMD, the lexicon has been heavily edited, rules have been adjusted and whole new compounding mechanism is added so that Estmorf would be suitable for using as a spelling check engine and analyser for real Estonian texts.

Another implementation has been created at the Institute of Estonian Language, based on the principles of open morphology (Viks, 2000). It is mostly an implementation of CMD with an added mechanism to allow analysis of compounds.

The third system is an FST-implementation of CMD that started its life as an experiment of describing Estonian with two-level morphology (Koskenniemi, 1983) in Heli Uibo's master's thesis (Uibo, 1999). It was then gradually extended with descriptions of some derivational processes by Heli Uibo (Uibo, 2005) and with complete dictionary of stems from CMD by Jaak Pruulmann-Vengerfeldt in his master's thesis (Pruulmann-Vengerfeldt, 2010). Also, some compounding rules were added and the whole FST was compiled of multiple smaller, specialized FSTs – there was a FST that described generation of simple word forms, another for simple-word exceptions that would override regular forms, a FST that described which of all possible concatenations of simple word forms are allowed as compounds etc. All those smaller FSTs were combined to a large final FST, that was able to generate and analyze word forms. There were a number of unsolved problems like the need to revise the dictionary similarly to what has been done for Estmorf, overgeneration because of weak compounding rules etc.

2.2.2 Adaptation

Oahpa is built on the Giellatekno infrastucture and so far all the morphology systems that have been in Oahpa have been FST-based. Thus, it was quite natural to try and adapt the existing FST-based system for Oahpa by integrating the existing FST into the Giellatekno infrastructure. This was useful for the other parts of the cooperation project that deal with machine translation as well. Also, the wider context of cooperation project motivates some of the decisions we made about FST.

For most languages, FST-s are described using a large lexicon FST (usually as Xerox lexc (Karttunen, 1993) source or at least something that is compiled to become a lexc source) and another FST to describe phonological processes using two-level rules. The Giellatekno infrastructure is well suited for such a structure and offers a comfortable set of supporting scripts and filters to generate a lot of specialized FSTs from the same source, if one follows some conventions. It is also worth mentioning that most active languages whose FST description is developed in Giellatekno infrastructure are close relatives to Estonian – multiple Saami languages, Finnish and now also Võro.

Our FST started out with a two-FST model. For various reasons, it was developed into a much more complicated system of FSTs. The source code of FSTs consisted of regular sources for automata and custom made build scripts that generated full source files from smaller parts, compiled binary FSTs from source and then combined those automata to get a final lexical transducer. In order to build our FST in the Giellatekno infrastructure, our first step was to reorganize our sources. Some of the reorganization meant that we precompiled some of the sources that were previously generated dynamically. Those build steps that combined small FSTs were merged into the Giellatekno infrastructure. The Giellatekno infrastructure is under active development to cater better to the needs of languages and applications that use language descriptions. The maintainers of Giellatekno infrastructure added necessary hooks, so that we could do some specialised processing between regular build steps of the Giellatekno infrastructure.

After we had managed to build our sources using the Giellatekno infrastructure and get a FST that worked more or less identically to what we had had before, the next step was to adapt our source. Mostly, this meant converting the tag set that was in use in the original FST to use the conventions used in Giellatekno. Tag adaptation had two aspects – most of the conversion was simple relabeling but in some instances the tag sets were not compatible or there were other reasons to consider bigger changes. Our existing tag system was mostly inspired by the structure that was dictated by CMD. Specific labels were chosen so that it would be as compatible with an existing constraint grammar syntax description of Estonian as possible. We suspect that Giellatekno's tag system has similar roots. The tag system is based on the first supported language descriptions and it has been extended and improved upon with the addition of new languages with somewhat different requirements. Most of the infrastructure and applications that depend on it have some adaptation to the existing Giellatekno tag set. We were also aware of the fact that the constraint grammar tools we were originally trying to interface with were about to be integrated into the Giellatekno infrastructure as well. So, it was decided that we would change tags at source level in all our rules and in our morphological lexicon. In addition to simple relabeling where the same thing was expressed with different tags (e.g. +in vs +Ine for inessive, +nom vs +Nom for nominative) there were some minor differences in the meaning of tags. For instance in our system we had separate tags for number (e.g. +pl, +sg) and person (e.g. +ps1, +ps2, +ps3) that were combined where needed as Giellatekno has precombined tags (e.g. +Sg1, +Pl2 for the first person singular and the second person plural, respectively).

One smaller part of tag relabeling was to convert uppercase letters that were used in two level rules to multichar tags so that uppercase letters could be used as a part of regular alphabet.

The sequence of tags in FSTs is as important as sequence of letters in a word. That means that in order to generate a specific word form with a generating FST, one usually has to know the lemma and the exact sequence of grammatical tags. The simplest form of rule-based machine translation would take a word form in source language, analyze it, replace the stem using translation dictionary and then try to generate the word using the same grammatical tags as the original analysis returned. Of course, the real languages are not that easy to translate and there are numerous more complicated rules but having the compatibility at that level is still a desirable property. As Oahpa needs to generate word forms as well, similar tag ordering rules for different languages are useful for developers and linguists who need to deal with multiple versions of Oahpa in parallel.

Our team members have studied languages that we have been prioritized for a machine translation subproject, that is North Saami and Finnish. Comparing different languages we realized that there is a lot of tradition involved in the ordering of tags in language descriptions. This means that even if there were a generic ordering that could be used for all languages involved, for historical reasons, it would be hard to enforce.

As a result of the analysis of different tagging conventions, the most notable change made to Estonian system was the restructuring of the tags for verb forms by Heiki-Jaan Kaalep theoretical foundations of which are described in (Kaalep, 2015). The aim of restucturing was to have a better match between grammatical meanings and specific surface forms that are used nowadays.

Another important difference between Giellatekno tradition and our previous FST was that in our original FST we automatically and dynamically generated regular derivations as if they were regular lemmas in the dictionary. For example, there are productive rules that derive name of action and actor from a verb (e.g. ujuma 'to swim' gives ujumine 'swimming' and ujuja 'swimmer'). Generating lemmas is not quite trivial as some of such derivations are based on weak-grade stem (e.g. lugema 'to read' and loetu 'something that has been read'). Some of our original more complicated system of FSTs dealt exactly with those derivations. However, Giellatekno infrastructure does not do such things but rather adds derivation-tags to mark that this word was derived from some base lemma using some specific derivation (loetu would be analyzed as *lugema+V+Der/tu+N+Sg+Nom* instead of *loetu+N+Sg+Nom* as before). It appeared that for disambiguation rules that kind of information is useful and so, in the current version we analyze (and generate) such derived words with both the synthetic lemma and original lemma with derivational tags. One of the future tasks is to analyze whether the synthetic lemma is really useful for any application or whether we could drop them and simplify our build system.

During the adaptation and testing of our FST with Oahpa, it appeared that our system did not have a good way to differentiate (partial) homonyms. There are quite a few paradigms that have exactly the same written form for nominative case forms, which is traditional the dictionary form for nouns and adjectives (e.g. sokk (nominative), soki (genitive) 'sock' vs sokk (nominative), soku (genitive) 'male goat'). This is often due to the loss of the final vowel in the nominative and such words actually inflect differently. For any application that needs to generate word forms by knowing the lemma and the grammatical information, that is of course a problem. So, to differentiate paradigms with overlapping nominative we used homonymy tags the Giellatekno tag set contains. This means that applications using our FSTs have to be aware of those tags as well, usually in the form of translation dictionaries having mapping not to the usual nominative but to the lemma with an additional identifier (e.g. sokk+Hom1 and sokk+Hom2).

The generic conclusion from the last two problems is that the lemma in the morphological module is actually an identifier of paradigm and as with other aspects of morphology module – what is useful and what makes sense depends somewhat on the intended users of the module.

The big problem of our current system is the overgeneration. The problem is largely a result of the mechanism of compounding. The current system combines the automaton of simple words with itself and then applies the filters that should only allow proper compounds and simple words. Such a structure enables us to add compounding relatively easily and deal with certain other problems that were hard to solve within our system of multiple automata. The current rules of compounding are too generic and there is a lot of allowed forms that actually are not used. Inclusion of some short words like names of musical notes in the lexicon makes this problem worse. Using a regular unweighted FST makes it also hard to prefer simple word analysis over compound word analysis.

The usual way to implement compounding rules in the Giellatekno infra would use diacritic flags as described in (Beesley and Karttunen, 2003) and cycles in lexicon description. Converting our system to use compounding mechanism that would be more in line with other language descriptions that use the Giellatekno infra is something that we have considered but have postponed so far. The most important reason for this is that there is no clear and formal description of compounding rules for Estonian. The gap between existing formal rules (e.g. a noun can be added to the nominative or genitive form of another noun) and what really is used (which of those two forms is preferred or if some combinations are used at all) is quite big and sometimes explained only by tradition.

As an experiment with flag diacritics we implemented rules for the lowercasing of proper name derivations. We found that the current system of filters makes the creative use of extra flags quite hard as the flags have to be precisely described in filters to show where exactly they can appear. Also, as flag diacritics are special and nontrivial to implement, they tend to cause problems that are hard to debug in both the filtering and composition of FSTs. One issue, for instance, is whether the negation of the whole alphabet contain flag diacritics in different implementations of FST tools or even in different operations in the same tool? What happens when we apply priority union [1] to FSTs with and without flag diacritics?

The other aspect of overgeneration is parallel forms. There are alternative forms of illative (long illative that uses regular morpheme and short illative that usually uses stem alteration, e.g. majasse vs majja 'into a house') with some preference rules for different inflection classes ('majja' is the preferred form but 'majasse' is understood as well). Some inflection classes also allow multiple forms for some plural cases (regular plural with morpheme vs plural stem, e.g. õpikutele vs õpikuile 'onto the textbooks'). Knowing all those forms is necessary for analysis but for generation in machine translation and for educational purposes it would be good to have only the preferred forms generated. Giellatekno infrastructure offers the tag +Use/NG to denote forms that are used but should not be generated for such purposes. We do have some experimental use of that flag but we still need to check and tag a lot of parallel forms either by word class or, in some cases, actually word by word.

2.3 Morphological FST of Võro

Võro, as is the situation with many of the other Uralic languages, has an abundance of regular morphology in both the nominal and verbal parts of speech. As such, ready solutions for many of the morphological challenges in Võro might be sought out in previous work done on the open-source, Saami language technology infrastructure "Giellatekno" in Tromsø, Norway. Morphophonological work at Giellatekno on the Saami languages has dealt with stem-internal vowel and consonant change as well as orthographical word compounding.

In the initialization of a new language at "Giellatekno", there are a number of default files for the development of two-level model and lexc descriptions. Concepts useful in the development morphophonological strategies and present in the default files include triggers and allophonic variables. Typically, triggers might be used in coordinating gradation in the stems, whereas allophonic variables might be utilized in progressive vowel harmony. There are, however, a few advanced languages to follow in development at Giellatekno, namely, Northern Saami, Southern Saami and Finnish. When in doubt these are the ones to quote and question because they are the scenes of most active development.

The morphophonological characteristics of Võro, at first glance, appear to be reminiscent of those attributed to Finnish. In addition to a parallel of the gradation system found in Estonian and Northern Saami, where changes in stem quantity and quality can be attested without apparent

[1] an operation on FSTs which allows us to declare and combine a large regular FST and a smaller one with some exceptions that override regular rules with much shorter descriptions than lexc-only descriptions would allow

surface-level motivation, Võro possesses progressive front-back vowel harmony. This said it was easy to find parallels on the Giellatekno infrastructure.

2.3.1 Initial approach to finite state description

Classification of the Võro language is available from Sulev Iva's dissertation (Iva, 2007) and online in the Võro-Estonian-Võro dictionary site `http://synaq.org`. Sulev Iva provided a digital copy of his word type classification lists, and work could be commenced.

In a parallel to previous lexc work on the Giellatekno infrastructure, inflection type names are simply words representative of the given type. Thus the inflection type name "VÕROKÕNÕ" 'a person from Võro' is used to distinguish nominals sharing its declension characteristics (cf. North and South Saami and Finnish). Since subsequent work often includes syntactic disambiguation, a part-of-speech indicator is prefixed onto the inflection type, which renders A_VÕROKÕNÕ, N_VÕROKÕNÕ and PROP_VÕROKÕNÕ continuation lexica that can be further directed to a mutual nominal lexicon in NMN_VÕROKÕNÕ (it is done similarly in the morphological FSTs of other Uralic languages such as Finnish, Livonian, Moksha, Hill Mari, Livvi, Skolt Saami and Nenets).

According to the initial description used for Võro, there are approximately 50 different declension groups (47 vs 53) and 40 conjugation groups (40 vs 36). The inflection groups contain words representative of both front and back vowel harmony, and therefore work was immediately begun on the description of progressive front-back vowel harmony.

In accordance with previous work on Mari, Erzya and certain Balto-Finnic languages a ready solution was reached for front-back vowel harmony. Two-level rules can deal with vowel harmony through the definition of vowel sets and contexts. In Võro this was initially accomplished through the definition of back, front and neutral vowels (1), and subsequent contexts (2).

```
(1)
VowBack = a o u \~{o};
VowFront = \"a \"o \"u ;
VowNeutral = e i ;
```

As is the case in Finnish, there is a set of neu-

no two-level rules are given for progressive vowel harmony.

The continuation lexica in the OMorFi Finnish description explicitly indicate both harmony and
tral vowels that do not block vowel harmony, in

gradation, and virtually leave the two-level rules unused. In practice this utilization of lexc doubles the number of inflection type lexica for those with vowel harmony targets, which, in the case of Finnish nouns, would comprise seven instances out of twelve. The illative in Finnish provides its own challenge, since it entails a duplication of the stem-final vowel, i.e. eight vowels. Gradation in Finnish centers on the plosives "k", "t" and "p", which is a small number in comparison to what is attested in Võro. These combinations are augmented by the need for expressing pluralia tantum, and the result is upward of 550 noun types (25.03.2015).

This is a good time to ask whether such a solution might be used in Võro, and whether it would be useful. First we have to ask ourselves what the transducers will be used for. If we are interested in ICALL, then we want intelligent feedback for our language learners.

Intelligent feedback can be written directly in the descriptions accompanying each inflection type. By establishing vowel harmony in an inflection type, we are providing the computer the necessary information needed to prompt the learner with regard to vowel harmony issues. We are looking into making information available at the lexicon level for computer reading. It is hoped that the information might be automatically added to individual words directed through a given lexicon, see (3).

```
(3)
(3.1) LEXICON N_PEREH
(3.2) ! pereh:perre
(3.3) ! vowel_harmony: front
(3.4) ! gradation: yes
(3.5) !! * Yaml: __N-pereh_gt-norm.yaml__
(3.6) :%^VowRM%>i FRONT_PL-GEN_de ;
(3.7) +Use/NG:%^WGStem%> h FRONT_PL-GEN_de ;
```

The declarations for vowel harmony at (3.1.3), and gradation at (3.1.4) are information bits that can be transferred to the ICALL infrastructure. In fact, it is the initial continuation lexicon associated with a given lemma and stem pair that makes reference to all this information, see "N_PEREH" in (3.1).

Hence the continuation lexicon "N_PEREH" in (4) is associated with the definition at LEXICON N_PEREH in (3.1), and attribute values can be added to the "<l>" element in (5). At the same time there is contemplation going on with regard to the use of well-documented triggers, such that the information from a single input line could be utilized by the computer for meaningful feedback. Such feedback in (3.1) might include "vowel loss" derived from the trigger "%^ VowRM". The trigger "%^ WGStem" would indicate "weak grade stem". Both would be associated with plural genitive in "de", as indicated expicitly in the continuation lexicon "FRONT_PL-GEN_de" at (3.1.6) and (3.1.7). The presence of the tag "+Use/NG" in (3.1.7) implies that the tagged sequence will be accepted by the analyzer but not generated.

```
(4)
pereh:perre N\_PEREH ;
```

Here the attribute values in the "<l>" element are hoped to be applied to the morphological games.

```
(5)
<e>
  <lg>
    <l gradation="yes" pos="N"
        vowel_harmony="front">
        pereh
    </l>
  </lg>
...
</e>
```

2.3.2 Brief assessment of progress

A happy medium is being sought for the intermingling of lexc and two-level rules strategies. Gradual progress is being made towards a lexc solution to vowel harmony, whereby word stems are classified for front-back harmony, so as to allow for immediate vowel-harmony error generation. Changes in the stem, however, are being worked on with triggers paralleling morphophonological rules such that wrong triggers can be applied in order to produce erroneous forms, according to strategies already developed for Northern Saami.

2.4 Pedagogical lexicons

We have used different approaches when composing the lexicons for Estonian and Võro Oahpa. The lexicon of Estonian Oahpa has been created on the basis of the word list of the Estonian textbook for beginners "E nagu Eesti" (Pesti and Ahi, 2011). The word list divided into the twenty-five chapters is given in the end of the textbook. It is a list of ca 1500 Estonian words and expressions with translations to English, Finnish, Russian and German.

We can bring out the following advantages and disadvantages of using a textbook's dictionary as a basis of Oahpa lexicon:

+ Book and chapter information are given, the lexicon can be easily used for additional grammar training in courses that base on that book. Translations of words to four most common languages of learners of Estonian exist.

- Information about part-of-speech and semantics had to be added manually or semi-automatically.

The creation of the Võro Oahpa lexicon started out with a small lexicon that had just one word for each inflection type. We have chosen this approach because we think it is important that the morphological exercises cover all the inflection types. We have tagged the representative words of inflection types so that exclusively these words can be chosen for the morphology drill exercise Morfa-S. Otherwise, the words are chosen from the full lexicon where some of the inflection types are less frequent and as the words are randomly selected there is a possibility that the user does not get a chance to practise some inflection types. After that we added ca 2500 words from the lexicon of North Saami Oahpa that incorporated translations to North Saami, Finnish, English, Norwegian (bokmål), Swedish and German.

Advantages and disadvantages of using an Oahpa lexicon of another language as a basis were the following:

+ Part-of-speech and "Oahpa-style" semantic information were already there, as well as translations to Finnish and English.

- The word list does not match the word list of any textbook of Võro, therefore this information must be added afterwards. Because it was a North Saami lexicon, it contained many words that were irrelevant for Võro (words about Saami handicraft, reindeering, also too strong focus on the topic "Christmas").

- Translations to Võro and Estonian had to be added.

3 Creation of the Oahpa applications for Estonian and Võro

Oahpa is a web application developed in Django framework. Django is a powerful open-source framework for creating web applications supporting the model-view-controller (MVC) design.

3.1 Setting up the Django application

As there has already been set up a number of instances of Oahpa for different languages in the Giellatekno infrastructure the process of creating Oahpa for Estonian and Võro was quite routine and did not require much effort. Obviously, each Oahpa instance has different settings – paths to linguistic tools, database access data, list of supported languages etc. We are aiming at having almost all the language-specific information in the settings file and in the database, rather than in the Python code. However, the Python code is still not entirely language-independent. A few adjustments were needed in the lists of grammatical and semantic categories, in the set of word attributes that come in from the lexicon, in the list of language pairs in the vocabulary drill game Leksa, in the list of localisation languages, in the initial settings of the games and in the spell-relax function.

3.2 Creation of the database

The complete database for an instance of Oahpa that incorporates Leksa, Morfa-S and Morfa-C (note that the program Numra is solely based on the finite state transductors converting the numerical, time and date expressions into textual form and vice versa) contains

- words, their translations and semantic classes
- tags used in the morphological analysis and their possible sequences (paradigms)
- word forms for Morfa-S
- question templates for Morfa-C linked to the word forms that can replace the variables in the templates
- morphological feedback information for each word form (this is combined from different characteristics and features of the word that gives hints about how to inflect the particular word)

We use a morphological generator to make the paradigms automatically. During the generation of the word forms and saving them into the database an error log is written to a file. So the database generation process also serves as testing of the morphological FST.

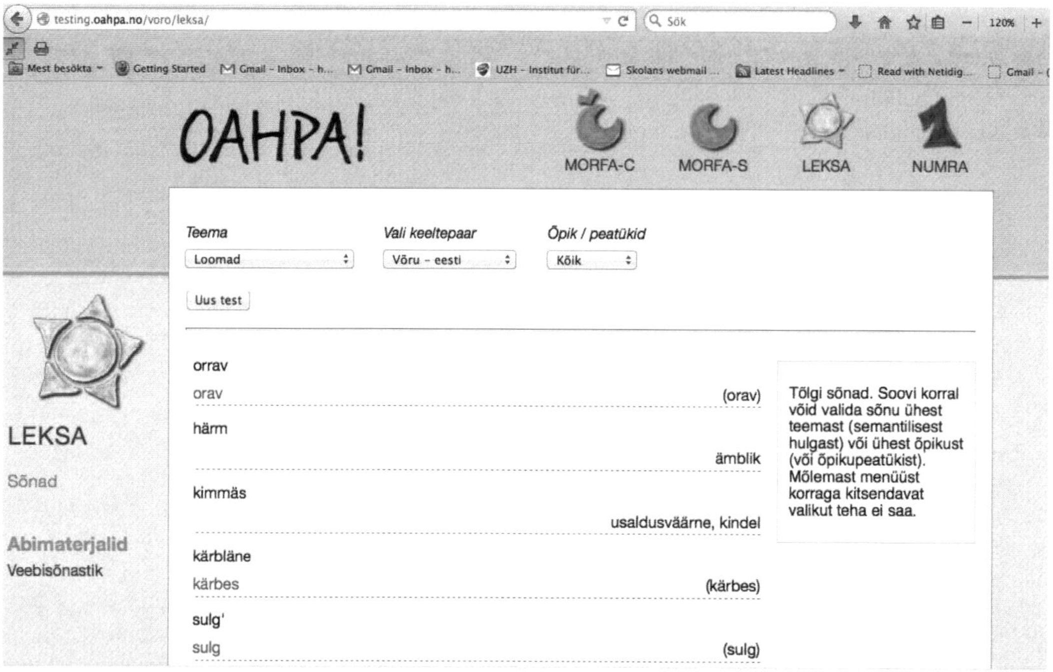

Figure 1: Screenshot of the vocabulary drill program Leksa in Võro Oahpa

So far we have set up Leksa, Morfa-S (substantives) and Morfa-C (substantives) for Estonian. The programs have been tested by the developers of FSTs and Oahpa and demonstrated to the teachers of Estonian at Tartu and Uppsala universities and at Estonian School in Stockholm for getting some feedback.

The working modules of Võro Oahpa are Numra, Leksa and Morfa-S (substantives and verbs). The user interfaces of both Estonian and Võro Oahpa have been translated to Estonian.

The user interface of Leksa in Võro Oahpa can be seen on Figure 1. There are three menus for specifying the exercise – *teema* ('topic', i.e. semantic category), *keeltepaar* ('language pair') and *Õpik / peatükid* ('book / chapters'). The first menu makes it possible to constrain the set of words offered to the user by semantics. On Figure 1 the words are chosen from the category *Loomad* ('animals'), for example *orrav* ('squirrel'), *härm* ('spider'), *kärbläne* ('fly'), *sulg'* ('feather'). There are 19 semantic categories in the list, among others family, food/drink, time, body, clothes, buildings/rooms, work/economy/tools. From the second pull-down menu the user can choose the language pair. The default is from Võro to the language of the user interface (in the given case – Estonian). Other translation languages in the list are Finnish, English, German, North Saami, Swedish and Norwegian. The correct answers of the user are displayed in green. In the second column the correct answers are presented by the system. The correct answer is given in parentheses if the user's answer is correct.

The current version of Estonian Oahpa can be tried out at the address `http://testing.oahpa.no/eesti` and Võro Oahpa at `http://testing.oahpa.no/voro`. The programs are free to use for everyone and do not require any registration.

3.3 Some problems and their solutions

3.3.1 Spell-relax

Spell-relax means that the program accepts different variants of typing for some characters or sequences of characters. This feature had been previously implemented in Oahpa in order to make Oahpa usable for users who do not have access to a keyboard (either virtual or real) with the layout of the language in focus.

We have not implemented any spell-relax in the Estonian Oahpa. We could perhaps consider accepting 'sh' instead of 'š' and 'zh' instead of 'ž' because it might be that everybody has not installed the Estonian keyboard but probably it would be a better idea to have a link to installation instructions of an Estonian keyboard. The written Estonian is highly normative and it would not be pedagogical to accept wrong spellings where for example the letters ä, ö, ü, õ are replaced by corresponding letters without diacritics. It is also important for the learner to capitalise proper names etc. where needed. Uppercase/lowercase mistakes are not tolerated.

The situation is quite different for the Võro language. We have implemented spell-relax in Võro Oahpa because the written language of Võro is relatively new and there is a big variety for how some phenomena are expressed. The things that are being spelled in various ways are not usual phonemes but rather symbols that mark a slightly different pronunciation:

1. palatalisation (conventionally denoted by modifier apostrophe, but all the other apostrophe-like characters are also accepted)
2. glottal stop (conventionally denoted by the letter 'q' but the use of 'q' is not consequent in the texts that are being published in the Võro language)

3.3.2 What is a correct word form?

As a developing language with multiple accepted forms, Võro may prove overwhelming for the beginner. For solely pedagogical purposes, it may prove necessary to limit the number of forms generated by the computer prompter to one given standard while allowing students the liberty of writing all possible forms. To this end the tag "+Use/NG", which has been used in MT previously at Giellatekno, can be used. Its use will provide form preference, something parallel to word preference already marked in the oahpa xml dictionaries with the "stat" attribute value "pref".

Should we accept some forms that are not normative but widely used? We might do it for Võro as the standarisation of this language is not finalised yet. The program should, however, suggest the normative form as the correct answer after it has accepted a widely used but non-normative form.

4 User groups of Estonian and Võro Oahpa and adaptation issues

The primary target group when designing Oahpa framework (that is, when developing the first version of the North Saami Oahpa in 2009-2011) were university students and other adult language learners who were learning North Saami as L2. The North Saami Oahpa has been integrated into the university courses at UiT. There are course pages with different kinds of materials for learning North Saami – texts with reading comprehension questions, recorded dialogues, grammar explanations, lexicons. When taking a university course in North Saami the students are working with Oahpa in the logged in mode that makes it possible for students to see their progress and for teachers and researchers to track the activity of the students, also they can see which topics in the course seem to be most difficult and hence should be given more attention. From the lessons there are direct links to appropriate drill exercises in Oahpa.

On the course pages `http://kursa.oahpa.no` and in North Saami Oahpa the scientific linguistic terminology is used and the grammar is explained on a level that is appropriate for its primary target group – adult learners. It should be noted, however, that some primary and secondary schools have also expressed an interest in using Oahpa. Since Oahpa is freely available on the Internet, it should be adapted to the wide user group – there should be possibilities to ask for help about difficult terms etc. That is why the developers of the North Saami Oahpa have introduced additional tooltip explanations of terms in Vasta and Sahka that pop up when pointing on a term in the error feedback. We plan to implement such help tooltips for Estonian Oahpa as well.

The target group of Võro Oahpa will be the students at the Võro language courses at University of Tartu. These are typically students of the Estonian language, thus they usually have a solid linguistic background.

The Estonian Oahpa will have three or four quite different user groups. The first group are the foreign students who have come to study at the University of Tartu and are taking a course in Estonian as L2. They will use Oahpa parallel to traditional language lessons in the classroom. The students have different mother tongues and are learning Estonian on the basis of English, Finnish or Russian. The University of Tartu Language Centre is organising these kinds of courses and plenty of students sign up for them each term.

The second group are students who take the

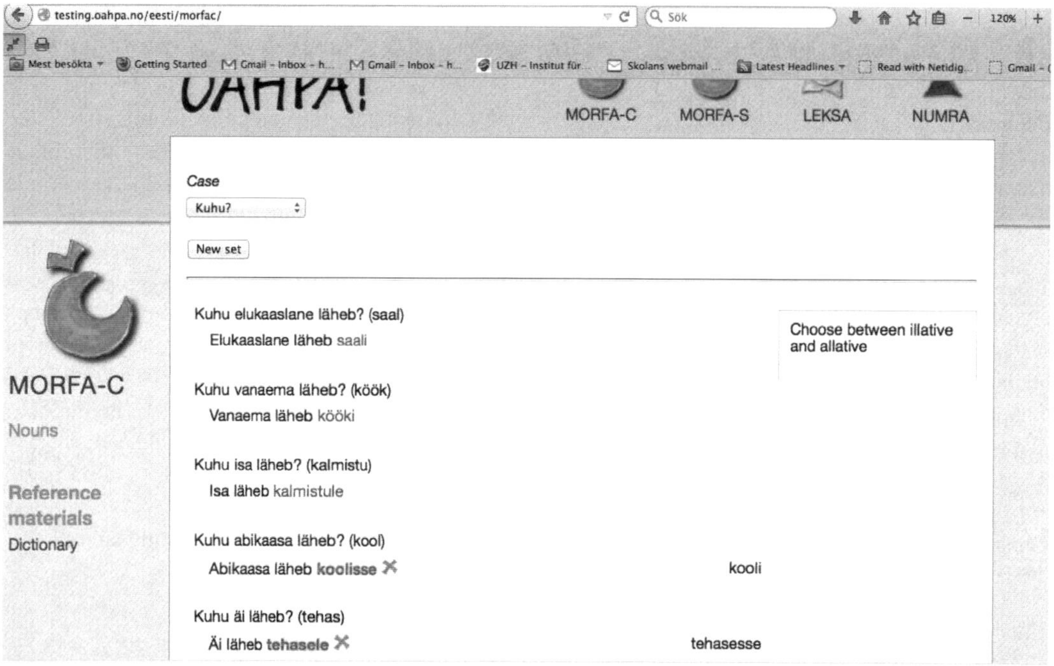

Figure 2: Screenshot of a more advanced Morfa-C exercise

web-based course in Estonian at Uppsala University in Sweden. The course that has been created by prof. Raimo Raag (Raag, 2010) is totally internet-based, the teachers meet their students only at video conferences. The course authors and teachers estimated Estonian Oahpa potentially useful for their students in achieving their vocabulary and grammar learning goals, given that some more exercise types will be implemented and links set from the lessons in the course materials to the relevant exercises in Oahpa.

The third group are the pupils at Estonian School in Stockholm (ESS). This is the only school in Sweden where Estonian language and culture are taught. The pupils in this school have different language backgrounds. Part of them have Estonian as their mother tongue and have recently moved from Estonia to Sweden, another part has lived in Sweden for a longer time and grown up in the Swedish language environment. Some pupils are grandchildren of Estonians who moved to Sweden in the 1940s. Another part of the pupils has no connection to the Estonian language at all.

Considering these different user groups we definitely have to make some adaptations, in particular for the young learners.

We have translated the lexicon of Estonian Oahpa to Swedish, for making Leksa usable for pupils at ESS. Leksa has been tested by the second grade pupils at this school and the feedback was positive. The teachers see the use of Leksa for learning both Estonian and Swedish. For young children with Estonian as the mother tongue and for Estonian as L2 learners Leksa may be used for training spelling of Estonian words. Estonian children who have recently moved to Sweden can also use Leksa for learning Swedish words.

Instead of international (Latin) case names that are generally not known to primary and secondary school students and because the school grammar books use Estonian case names, we are using case questions (e.g. *kelle?* "whose" *Omastav* "Genitive" instead of *Genitiiv*) and Estonian case names.

Led by the feedback of university teachers we have deviated from the standard setup of case list in Estonian Morfa-C. Instead of always explicitly giving the case we have implemented some exercises which include a choice between two grammatical forms. For example, in the exercise "Kuhu?" 'Where (to)?' the student must choose between illative and allative. An example screenshot of this exercise is presented on Figure 2.

The Estonian language teachers at ESS have also given some other ideas for Morfa-C exercises that are on the waiting list of implementation: choosing the object case, choosing the correct infinitive form (there are two infinitives in Estonian – da-infinitive and ma-supine – the usage of which in a given context is difficult for non-natives) and more. These are examples of exercises that are well supported by the Oahpa framework and easy to implement.

Another possibility to adapt the same instance of Oahpa to different user groups is to have the choice between different sources of words. Both Leksa and Morfa-S have the corresponding menu 'book' in their user interface. Lexicons, word lists of textbooks, single chapters or groups of book chapters can be listed in this menu.

For teaching the university course of Estonian as a foreign language the textbook "E nagu Eesti" (Pesti and Ahi, 2011) is used both at the University of Tartu and Uppsala University.

We are also planning to add the dictionaries of the Estonian textbooks used at the Estonian language courses at ESS into the Oahpa lexicon. The same textbooks are also used at Russian schools in Estonia and the Estonian school in Riga.

One of the initial ideas when designing Oahpa was that only "the known" words (words that occur in the textbook's word list and also in the vocabulary drill program Leksa) will be used in grammar exercises. We will make it more fine-grained. According to feedback from the teachers of Estonian it is important that beginners' grammar exercises would not contain too advanced vocabulary. Thus, there is a new detail in the Morfa-C question frames for Estonian – not only the semantic class but also the book chapter where the word is introduced is determined when selecting words for a particular grammar exercise.

Some of the vocabulary can also be unknown because of cultural differences. For example food differs quite a lot even between otherwise culturally quite similar countries Estonia and Sweden. People who have not grown up in Estonia may wonder what *ühepajatoit* (a typical Estonian late summer / autumn hot pot usually made of pork, carrot, turnip and cabbage) or *rosolje* (a Russian beet root salad) is. We still think that learning a language cannot be separated from getting acquainted with the culture. Probably, these words are not appropriate in the exercises meant for absolute beginners but they could come a bit later.

5 Conclusions and future work

The use of FSTs for morphological analysis and generation and standardised XML formats to store lexicon and exercise frames makes it possible to effectively create a variety of morphological drills for learners of morphologically complex languages.

Our experiments with setting up language learning system for two new languages – Estonian and Võro – prove that the method that has been worked out at Giellatekno research group in Tromsø is efficient and makes it possible to create the first prototypes of vocabulary and morphology drill modules with a relatively small effort. The obligatory prerequisites for creating such a system are a lexicon that can just be a word list of the course textbook in the pdf format and the morphological FST that will be used for generating all the inflection forms of the words in the lexicon.

The major work that has to be done is the work in developing the morphological FST. At the same time, the FST in itself is a multi-purpose building block that can be used in a variety of applications as for example spelling check, machine translation and an intelligent dictionary.

In our case, we had to create the Võro FST from scratch. Despite that, we could start developing the language learning system in parallel with that and very soon come up with a prototype of the morphology drill program that just contained one representative from each inflection type.

There existed a "beta version" of FST for Estonian that had to be restructured somewhat in order to accommodate it in the Giellatekno infrastructure.

The pedagogical applications also set some additional constraints on the FST. It is usual that some of the parallel forms and infrequent words have to be excluded from the pedagogical FST. Here, once again, the Giellatekno infrastructure already had a solution that we could apply.

The described systems are in the middle of development but as the feedback from teachers has been positive we feel optimistic about continuing the work on both Estonian and Võro finite state transducers and the respective Oahpa instances where with first of all plan to complete Morfa-S and Morfa-C with other inflectable word classes.

It is also important to add more guidelines and error feedback to the systems. We are going to use the same approach as in North Saami where the feedback of morphological forms is combined from pieces of information that characterise the inflection type of the given word. This approach is described in (Antonsen, 2012) and (Antonsen et al., 2013).

References

Lene Antonsen, Saara Huhmarniemi, and Trond Trosterud. 2009. *Interactive pedagogical programs based on constraint grammar*. Proceedings of the 17th Nordic Conference of Computational Linguistics. Nealt Proceedings Series 4.

Lene Antonsen. 2012. *Improving feedback on L2 misspellings – an FST approach*. Proceedings of the SLTC 2012 workshop on NLP for CALL, Lund, 25th October, 2012. Linköping Electronic Conference Proceedings 80: 1-10.

Lene Antonsen, Ryan Johnson, Trond Trosterud, and Heli Uibo. 2013. *Generating modular grammar exercises with finite-state transducers*. Proceedings of the second workshop on NLP for computer-assisted language learning at NODALIDA 2013, May 22-24, Oslo, Norway. NEALT Proceedings Series 17: 27-38.

Kenneth R. Beesley and Lauri Karttunen. 2003. *Finite State Morphology*. CSLI publications in Computational Linguistics, USA.

Sulev Iva. 2007. *Võru kirjakeele sõnamuutmissüsteem 'Inflectional Morphology in the Võro Literary Language'*. PhD Thesis. Tartu Ülikooli Kirjastus, Tartu, Estonia.

Heiki-Jaan Kaalep. 2015. Eesti verbi vormistik. 'Estonian verb paradigm' *Keel ja Kirjandus 1/2015:* 1–16. Eesti Teaduste Akadeemia ja Eesti Kirjanike Liidu ajakiri. SA Kultuurileht, Tallinn, Estonia.

Heiki-Jaan Kaalep and Tarmo Vaino. 2000. Teksti täielik morfoloogiline analüüs lingvisti töövahendite komplektis. 'The complete morphological analysis of the text in the toolbox of a linguist.' *Arvutuslingvistikalt inimesele. Tartu Ülikooli üldkeeleteaduse õppetooli toimetised:* 87–99. Tartu Ülikooli Kirjastus, Tartu, Estonia.

Lauri Karttunen. 1993. *Finite-State Lexicon Compiler*. Technical Report. ISTL-NLTT-1993-04-02. April 1993. Xerox Palo Alto Research Center. Palo Alto, California.

Kadri Koreinik. 2013. The Võro language in Estonia. ELDIA Case-Specific Report. *Studies in European Language Diversity 23*. (Ed.) Johanna Laakso Research consortium ELDIA c/o Prof. Dr. Anneli Sarhimaa, Northern European and Baltic Languages and Cultures (SNEB), Johannes Gutenberg-Universität Mainz.

Kimmo Koskenniemi. 1983. *Two-level Morphology: A General Computational Model for Word-Form Recognition and Production*. PhD Thesis. University of Helsinki.

Sjur Moshagen, Jack Rueter, Tommi Pirinen, Trond Trosterud, and Francis M. Tyers. 2014. Open-Source Infrastructures for Collaborative Work on Under-Resourced Languages *Proceedings of CCURL (Collaboration and Computing for Under-Resourced Languages in the Linked Open Data Era) workshop 2014 organised with LREC2014:* 71–77 European Language Resources Association (ELRA).

Mall Pesti, and Helve Ahi. 2011. *E nagu Eesti. Eesti keele õpik algajaile 'E as Estonia. Estonian for beginners'*. TEA Kirjastus, Tallinn, Estonia.

Jaak Pruulmann-Vengerfeldt. 2010. *Praktiline lõplikel automaatidel põhinev eesti keele morfoloogiakirjeldus 'Practical Finite State Morphology of Estonian'*. M.Sc. Thesis. Tartu Ülikool, Tartu, Estonia.

Raimo Raag. 2010. Den språkliga mångfalden – småspråkens renässans. (Ed.) Jenny Lee *Kunskapens nya världar, Uppsala: Uppsala Learning Lab, Uppsala universitet:* 211–221.

Trond Trosterud and Heli Uibo. 2005. Consonant Gradation in Estonian and Sami: Two-Level Solution. (Eds) Antti Arppe et al. *Inquiries into Words, Constraints and Contexts:* 136–150.

Heli Uibo. 1999. *Eesti keele sõnavormide arvutianalüüs ja -süntees kahetasemelist morfoloogiamudelit rakendades. 'The computerized analysis and synthesis of Estonian word forms using the two-level morphology model'*. M.Sc. Thesis. Tartu Ülikool, Tartu, Estonia.

Heli Uibo. 2005. Finite-State Morphology of Estonian: Two-Levelness Extended. (Ed R. Mitkov) *Proceedings of the International Conference on Recent Advances in Natural Language Processing (RANLP) 2005:* 580–584. Borovets.

Ülle Viks. 1992. *A concise morphological dictionary of Estonian: introduction & grammar*. Estonian Academy of sciences, Institute of language and literature.

Ülle Viks. 2000. Eesti keele avatud morfoloogiamudel. 'An open morphology model of Estonian' *Arvutuslingvistikalt inimesele. Tartu Ülikooli üldkeeleteaduse õppetooli toimetised:* 9–36. Tartu Ülikooli Kirjastus, Tartu, Estonia.

Shuly Wintner. 2008. Strengths and weaknesses of finite-state technology: a case study in morphological grammar development. *Natural Language Engineering 14(4)*:457-469. Cambridge University Press.